李阳·克立兹

英语听力突破掌上宝(上册)

李阳·克立兹　编著

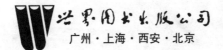

世界图书出版公司

广州·上海·西安·北京

李阳·克立兹

　　为实现"让三亿中国人说一口流利的英语！"和"让中国之声响彻全世界！"的理想而奋斗终身！

作者简介

* * *

李阳祖籍山西，1969 年出生于祖国大西北的新疆乌鲁木齐。其父母六十年代大学毕业后响应党的号召志愿支援边疆建设。李阳中学的学习状况不很理想，1985 – 1986 年高三期间因对学习失去信心曾几欲退学，1986 年自新疆实验中学勉强考入兰州大学工程力学系。大学一二年级李阳多次补考英语。为了彻底改变英语学习失败的窘况，李阳开始奋起一搏，他摒弃了偏重语法训练和阅读训练的传统，另辟蹊径，从口语突破，并独创性将考试题变成了朗朗上口的句子，然后脱口而出。经过四个月的艰苦努力，李阳在 1988 年大学英语四级考试中一举获得全校第二名的优异成绩。

李阳还和同学合作，用自己的方法进行同声翻译训练，达到了在别人讲话的同时，可以在只落后一、两句的情况下立刻翻译成英语的程度。李阳更是提出了全新的、简单的翻译标准，他称之为“中国人说中国话”，只要你是一个受过基础教育的中国人，你就可以成为一个出色的翻译。李阳从大学四年级开始便广泛地参与了大量的国内和国际场合的口译。

在此基础上，李阳摸索总结出一套独特的以一个非英语专业的英语学习失败者为基点的英语学习法，集“听说读写译”于一体，人称“疯狂英语”，在发音、口语、听力和口译上卓有成效。疯狂英语将英语的素质教育和传统的考试完美地结合。1989 年李阳首次成功地战胜了自我，公开发表演讲介绍这套方法，并开始应邀到各大、中学校传授疯狂英语。多年来，运用这套方法的大、中学生更是创造了托福、四六级和高考成绩大幅提高的惊人奇迹。

1990 年李阳大学毕业被分配到西安西北电子设备研究所当了一年半助理工程师，从事军事和民用卫星地面站工作。这一年中他坚持每天清晨在单位九楼顶大喊英、法、德、日语，进一步实践和完善了“疯狂英语突破法”。

1992 年，李阳因出色的英语水平被调入广州筹办中国第一家省级英语电台——广东人民广播电台英文台，并担任新闻播音员和“TALKSHOW”（脱口秀）节目主持人，同时主持广州电视台的英语新闻节目，是广州地区最受欢迎的英语播音员。

李阳用其独创的方法练就了一口连美国人都难以分辨的地道美语，他配音的广告在香港和东南亚电视台广泛播送。同时，他也是广州著名的独立口译员、双语主持人和美国总领事馆文化处、农业处和商务处的特邀翻译，被人誉为“万能翻译机”，圆满地完成了各种大型国际会议、谈判和外事访问的口译任务。例如在中美关系处于紧张状态的一九九三年底,李阳担任了美国众议院外交委员会首席顾问理查德·布什先生关于"克林顿当选总统以来美国对华政策的制订过程"重要演讲的现场口译,获得了中美双方的高度赞赏,会后收到美国外交委员会的特别感谢信。

李阳独立完成的主要口译还有大家熟悉的信息高速公路、移动通讯、知识产权保护、电脑软件保护、最惠国待遇问题、关贸总协定、国际环境保护、公司法和证券等等专题的演讲、国际研讨会和国际电视电话会议。

李阳纯正的美国英语引起不少外国记者的好奇,美国的 ABC 广播网、英国的 BBC、香港电台(RTHK)、日本放送协会(NHK)、苏格兰国家电视一台以及加拿大国际广播电台等都曾采访过他。

1994 年,李阳辞去在广东电台的工作,创办李阳·克立兹国际英语推广工作室,全身心投入"在中国普及英文、向世界传播中文"的事业。迄今为止已经在全国各地义务讲学一千多场次,听讲人数近千万人。他的奉献精神,赢得了民族工业的鼎力支持,在企业的赞助下,李阳向全国赠送了五百多万套学习卡,为革命老区培训师资并赠送了二十多万元的学习资料。李阳的讲学集爱国主义教育、人生激励和科学快捷的教法与学法于一体。他那发奋进取、百折不挠的传奇经历、强烈的爱国主义激情和极富感召力的卓越口才构成了他独特的人格魅力,鼓舞着千千万万的英语学习者迈上了语言和人生的成功之路,在更高层次、更深意义上掀起了中国空前的征服英语热潮。

李阳打破国际上语言课小班的惯例,数千人甚至数万人一起上课。香港和东南亚的华人慕名来广州接受他的培训。新加坡、日本、台湾和泰国的大公司、学院和培训机构纷纷邀请李阳前往讲学。李阳的方法同样适合于外国人学习中文。他的学生已经在美国、新西兰、日本等国家开设了"疯狂英语"、"疯狂中文"培训课程。中国人走向世界传播中文和中国文化的时代已经到来!

国内外一百多家报纸、杂志,数十家电视台、广播电台都报道了李阳的事迹和方法,由于他在英语教育和人生激励方面的卓越贡献,国内外传媒和广大英语学习者称誉他为"英语播种机"和"人生激励导师"。疯狂英语风靡全国。

"激发爱国热情、弘扬民族精神;攻克英语、振兴中华"李阳·克立兹覆盖中国一千城市、三亿英语学习者的大型全国巡回演讲已经拉开序幕。与此同时,致力于将疯狂英语学习法融入大中小学英语教育、为国家培养实用实战型人才的工程也开始启动。

李阳将继续以自己的不懈奋斗,为中国和世界的外语教学和文化交流作出更大的贡献!

本套书附录音带2卷

录音带上只录有本套书部分主要内容，因为李阳·克立兹认为只要听烂一盒录音带听力就可以完全过关，每一句话都配录音是没有必要的，也会增加学习者的经济负担。

李阳·克立兹
英语听力突破掌上宝（上册）

李阳·克立兹　编著

广东世界图书出版公司出版

东莞新丰彩印公司印刷

广东世界图书出版公司发行　　各地新华书店经销

广州市新港西路大江冲25号

邮政编码：510300

电话：020－84451969

1997年12月第一版　开本787×1092　1/32

1998年8月第5次印刷　印张4.375

印数：61001～71000

ISBN 7－5062－3181－6/H·0066

出版社注册号：粤014

定价：25.00元（上下册）

目　录

1

（手写）1(1) → 66(A)
1(2) P68
2(1) 66-86(B)
709 小对话 P68
2(2) 128A

我 的 自 述

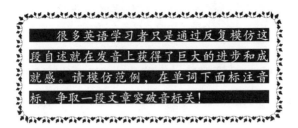

很多英语学习者只是通过反复模仿这段自述就在发音上获得了巨大的进步和成就感。请模仿范例，在单词下面标注音标，争取一段文章突破音标关！

Hi, this is Li Yang. I graduated from Lanzhou
[ˈgrædʒueit]
University and majored in Mechanical Engineering. I

was once a poor student of English, and it was my

biggest headache and trouble-maker. I got sick and

tired of learning boring grammar rules and lifeless
[ˈlaiflis]
words. But through hard work in practicing speaking

English and breaking away from the traditional
[trəˈdiʃənl]
grammar games, I found myself a totally different

and exciting new world. Not only did I pass Band 4
[ikˈsaitiŋ]
and Band 6 College English exams very easily with

high marks, but more importantly, I began to use

English.

1

Finally, I developed a new Language Cracking System myself. I began to teach German not long after I started to learn this terribly difficult language in my own way. It was a miracle but I made it. To ['mirəkl] speak good English, I think one year of study should be enough for any diligent and intelligent person.

I'd like to share my learning techniques with you, and I will be very glad to answer your letters and be your friend.

第 一 章

口语突破听力
口语听力共同辉煌之疯狂原则

疯 狂 原 则

世界上其实根本不存在听力的问题！听力的真正突破是以口语突破为基础的，孤立的、"默默无闻"的为听而听的听力训练存在巨大弊端并且极其低效。克立兹方法告诉你：你一定能听懂你能说出的东西！你只管去大量地练习说，只要发音纯正、用法地道，你的听力必将一日千里！而且你采用的是超级"三最"口腔肌肉训练法，你比外国人说得还要快，难道还怕听不懂吗？现代化的语言实验室和磁带将退居二线！

如何做到发音纯正

只要注意发音五大秘诀，然后再模仿一盘地道美音的磁带，发音就可以完全过关！有关发音的详细阐述请参阅《李阳·克立兹对发音的最后宣战——英语发音突破掌上宝》。

3

如何做到用法地道

刚开始的时候，要注意选择地道的教材，刻苦模仿，养成良好的地道英语习惯。更重要的是，要学会"时时刻刻处处"收集地道的句子，用三最法彻底将它们"私有化"，逐步改造自己的中国式英语，逐步增强自己的地道英语表达能力。

我印象最深的一个地道表达法是 *care for*，是在一次偶然的交谈中学到的，我通过国外的字典和教材收集了以下五个句子，使这个动词短语成为我脱口而出的朋友！以后一听到这个短语，我立刻就会有反应，因为我自己也经常用 *care for*！

* *Do you care for this kind of music? Personally, I don't like jazz.*
* *I read the novel last night, but I didn't care for it at all.*
* *The poetry is very realistic. I don't care for it very much.*

  （这首诗是写实的，我不太喜欢。）
* *Would you care for a cup of tea?*
* *I don't really care for tea; I like coffee better.*

最 高 境 界

说话、阅读等于练习听力

　　就像你的母语，你已经不用再购买磁带，只要是你说过的东西、读过的东西，你肯定能够听懂！这就是我能够轻松听懂美国电影、听懂广播电视、听懂专业讲座的原因。因为我的发音地道，我的语感良好，就像外国人一样，所以只要是我读过的东西，我就能够听懂！于是我只要把美国电影的剧本、广播电视新闻的新闻稿、专业报告的文字材料大声朗读一遍，我就可以毫不费力地听懂！英语是我的第二母语！

阅读练听力是我能胜任各类口译的秘密武器！

　　有这样一块空白的地方，我想再送给您一个漂亮的句子，下次见面时和我比赛一下，看谁说得又快又标准！

　❋ *You made the most of your three days in Paris. I think you saw everything there.*

　【注】make the most of something = do the best one can in a situation; get as much as possible out of it：尽量利用；获得最大利益。

第二章

李阳·克立兹句子处理
"疯狂三步曲"

现在让我们来做第一步：疯狂地收集地道句子，疯狂地脱口而出！下面是和一个句子建立深厚感情的三个步骤：

1、把收集到的地道句子全部换成第一人称，想像那些事情就发生在你自己身上或自己周围！

2、然后用"三最"法"恶狠狠"地喊若干遍，直至脱口而出！

3、最后以标准的语速和自然的语调充满深情地、得意地说一遍！就像是一个外国人正在讲这句话，同时脑海中想像一下这句话所描述的具体情景！然后举一反三，活学活用，彻底私有化。

到这里就算基本上掌握这个句子了，以后遇到类似的句型就会像母语一样立刻反应，小菜一碟。这个立刻反应是指立刻脱口而出，听懂当然就更没有问题了！李阳·克立兹英语口语突破法就是英语听力突破法！听力在我们这里根本不成问题！

示范一：**They would have come to the meeting if they had known about it.**

（他们如果知道这个会议就会来参加了。）[C]

[A] Although they knew there was going to be a meeting, they didn't come.

[B] They didn't want to attend the meeting, but they did anyway.

[C] They didn't know about the meeting.

[D] They didn't let anybody know about the meeting, so nobody attended.

第一步: 改装如下:

I would have come to the meeting if I had known about it.

第二步: "三最"。李阳·克立兹的记录是:2秒。

第三步: 深情;含糊地说一遍。然后想像在什么情况下可以把这个句子卖弄出去。比如:为什么技术科的同志/他们/你的父母没有来参加会议?这时你可以自豪地脱口而出这句"虚拟语气"的句子,这是多么了不起!

特别注意: 在四个供选择的答案中虽然有三个是错的,但这三个错的答案同样是地道的英文,也可以用上面的三个步骤进行处理。也就是说这道题包含了五笔财富!

* * * * * * * * * * *

示范二:John was supposed to arrive at 6:15, but he's an hour and a half late. (约翰应该六点一刻到,但他晚了一个半小时。)[C]

[A] The time is now 6:45.

[B] The time is now 7:15.

[C] The time is now 7:45.

[D] The time is now 7:20.

第一步：改装如下：

> I was supposed to arrive at 6: 15, but I'm an hour and a half late.

第二步："三最"。李阳·克立兹的记录是：3秒。一分钟可以读 20 遍。

第三步：深情、含糊地说一遍。然后想像在什么情况下可以把这个句子卖弄出去。比如：当你约会的人让你足足等了一个半小时，你可以冲着他/她生气加自豪地脱口而出这个高级精品句，多了不起，因为你正确地使用了 be supposed to！

* Every student is supposed to know the school regulations.

　（每个学生都应该知道校规。）

* The program was supposed to begin at 9 o'clock, but the president's speech delayed it 20 minutes.

　= The program began at 9:20.

* * * * * * * * * * * *

示范三： **John must have forgotten about our meeting.**

（约翰一定忘记了我们的会议了。）[B]

[A] John never forgets when he has a meeting.

[B] It seems that John forgot about our meeting.

[C] John should have cancelled the meeting.

[D] John has to come to the meeting.

第一步：改装如下：

> Mom must have forgotten about my birthday.

第二步："三最"。李阳·克立兹的记录是：1.5秒。

第三步：深情、含糊地说一遍。然后想像一下这句话所描述的情景：大家在开会，但唯独约翰没有来，于是进行了猜测。然后再接着想像在什么情况下可以把这个句子卖弄出去。我立刻把大脑开动起来，想出以下几个句子：

* She must have been beautiful when she was young.（她年轻时一定很漂亮。）【高级精品句】

* He must have told a lie.（他一定说了谎。）

* John must have been exhausted after that run.
  = John was probably very tired after running.

＊　＊　＊　＊　＊　＊　＊　＊　＊　＊　＊

示范四：It's not like Ted to be late for an appointment, so I don't know what's keeping him.

（迟到可不是泰德的作风，我不知道是什么事情耽搁了他。）[C]

[A] Ted pointed out where the key was.

[B] Ted doesn't want to be appointed.

[C] Ted is usually a punctual person.

[D] Ted doesn't know he has an appointment.

第一步：改装。其实只需将名字换一下就可以马上用了。

第二步："三最"。李阳·克立兹的记录是：3 秒。

第三步：深情、含糊地说一遍。然后想像在什么情况下可以把这个句子卖弄出去。比如：老板/老师/自己的好朋友是个非常守时的人，但某一天却来晚了，于是你脱口而出上面这个漂亮的句子。

＊　＊　＊　＊　＊　＊　＊　＊　＊　＊　＊

示范五：W: Hi, Bob. Come on in. I'm glad you could make it to the party this evening. But where's Jane?

M: She sends you her apologies. She has a big exam tomorrow and wants to be sure she's ready for it.

（她向你表示道歉。明天她有一个大考试，她想准备充分一点。)

Q: What's Jane doing this evening?

A: Studying for an exam.

第一步：改装。这个对话里的句子可以分开改装使用。当别人应邀参加你的晚会时，你可以说：Come on in. I'm glad you could make it to the party this evening. 当代替别人致歉时，可以说：She sends you her apologies. 当别人请你去看电影／吃饭／聚会，而你因为要考试不能去时，可以说：I have a big exam tomorrow and want to be sure I'm ready for it.

一个小对话里的"财富"可以使我在三个不同场合潇洒地脱口而出！可见"改装"和"私有化"能力在学习英语中是多么重要！在学习完李阳·克立兹教材以后，就应该熟练地掌握了改装能力和技巧，并养成了随时随地改装的习惯。

第二步："三最"。李阳·克立兹的记录是：9秒。

第三步：深情、含糊地说一遍。然后想像在什么情况下可以把这些句子卖弄出去。

* * * * * * * * * * * *

示范六：**Peter always has got a lot of good ideas but he rarely follows them through to completion.**

（彼得常常有很多好主意，但他很少善始善终／经常半途而废。）

= He doesn't usually finish what he starts.

第一步：改装。我以前也是这样的，但现在有点改进，所以这个句子可以改装成 I used to have a lot of good ideas but I rarely followed them through to completion.

第二步："三最"。李阳·克立兹的记录是：3秒。

第三步：深情、含糊地说一遍。然后想像在什么情况下可以

把这个句子卖弄出去。比如：你的好朋友/同事/你
父亲就是这样一类人，你可以用上面的句子评价他
们。下面再给大家一个句子，以便掌握"善始善终"
这个成语：

＊ He followed the plan through to the end.
（他把那计划贯彻到底。）

＊　＊　＊　＊　＊　＊　＊　＊　＊　＊　＊　＊

示范七：**The professor was so lost** 『忘形的；入迷的』 **in
thought that he missed his stop.**〔D〕

[A] He missed the bus because he lost his way.

[B] He thought a lot about losing his job.

[C] He thought he was lost, so he stopped driving.

[D] He passed his stop because he wasn't paying
attention.

第一步：改装如下：

I was so lost in thought that I missed my stop.

第二步："三最"。李阳·克立兹的记录是：2.5秒。

第三步：深情、含糊地说一遍。然后想像在什么情况下可以
把这个句子卖弄出去。教授和学者好像是这个句
子的主要对象，因为他们总是若有所思。我也常
常坐过站，不是因为入迷和忘形，而是因为太累
睡着了。

＊　＊　＊　＊　＊　＊　＊　＊　＊　＊　＊　＊

示范八：**Before the class began, a dozen students were
in the room, but soon the number doubled.**

= There were 24 students in the class after it had
begun.

第一步：改装如下：

11

Before the meeting/lecture/speech began, a dozen people were in the room, but soon the number doubled.

第二步："三最"。李阳·克立兹的记录是：2.5秒。

第三步：深情、含糊地说一遍。然后想像在什么情况下可以把这个句子卖弄出去。

* * * * * * * * * * * *

示范九：W: **Did you hear that the neighborhood convenience store was held up last night?**

M: **Yes, I heard it on the radio this morning.**

Q: **What happened at the convenience store last night?**

A: **There was a robbery『抢劫』.**

第一步：改装。当向别人讲述事件的时候，可以用：Did you hear that ...；当告诉别人消息来源时，可以用：I heard it on the radio this morning. 而且还学会了两个可以卖弄的重要说法：neighborhood convenience store(社区便利店)和 hold up(抢劫)。

第二步："三最"。李阳·克立兹的记录是：7秒。

第三步：深情、含糊地说一遍。然后想像在什么情况下可以把这个句子卖弄出去。这个对话我经常用，因为95、96年广东发生了数次重大恶性抢劫杀人案件。

下面给大家几个实用的句子财富：

* The building of the new road has been held up by bad weather.

（这条新路的建设因坏天气而耽搁了。）

* The gunman held up the passengers and took all their money.

（这名枪手洗劫了乘客。）

* * * * * * * * * * * * *

示范十：M：I'd love to see a different type of movie for a change. I'm tired of movies about prison breaks 『越狱』and insane 『疯狂的；患精神病的；非常愚蠢的；毫无见识的』asylums 『精神病院；收容所；避难所』.【一词多译，苦练中英文自由转换能力】

（我想换换口味，看一种不同类型的电影。我厌倦了关于越狱和疯人院的片子。）

W：I agree; let's go to see the new movie at the Center Theater. I hear it's a realistic and touching story of two young lovers.

（我同意。让我们去中央剧院看一部关于两个年轻恋人现实而感人的故事片吧。）【高级精品句】

Q：What kind of movie does the man not want to see?

A：One about jail escapes and mental hospitals.

第一步：改装。上面那段对话，我相信很多人都会有同感。现在社会上的人已经不知道应该如何去消遣，关于色情、暴力、变态的电视和电影充斥社会，造成了恶劣的影响。我相信人们还是热爱美好上进的事物，也需要这些美好的东西来净化人们的思想、陶冶人们的情操。

上面这个对话几乎不用改装，就可以马上卖弄，"据为己有"。

第二步："三最"。李阳·克立兹的记录是：14秒。

第三步：深情、含糊地说一遍。然后想像在什么情况下可以把这个对话卖弄出去。比如：你和你的朋友去看电影、去借录像带、光碟等等。

下面再送给大家十个句子和对话，自己去进行上面的三个步骤：

1. **It's amazing how much the boy takes after『像；相似』his father.**

   = Father and son are very much alike『相像』.

2. **There was so little traffic that Stone got home from work in half of the usual time.**

   （交通顺畅，史东只用了平常一半的时间就到家了。）

   = Stone took half as long to get home.

3. **The nurse suggested that he rest for half an hour before going back to work.**

   = The nurse said he should take a break before returning to work.

4. **I would have driven to the theater last night, but it's always so difficult to find a parking place.**

   = I didn't drive.

5. **Little did she imagine that I passed the history course.**

   = She didn't imagine that I passed the history course.

❋ ❋ ❋ ❋ ❋ ❋

6. W: **This room is so stuffy, I can hardly breathe.**

   M: **I think they should ban smoking here, don't you?**

   Q: **Why is the woman complaining?**

   A: **Too many people are smoking.**

7. W: **Professor Stone helped me so much that I'm thinking of buying him a book of poetry.**

   M: **I think you should get him a record. Just because he's an English teacher doesn't mean that all he does is read.**

   Q: **What does the man mean?**

   A: **People who teach English like things besides books.**

8. W: How about phoning Liz and asking her to join us for dinner.

   M: I think you should phone her, she hardly knows who I am.

   Q: What does the man mean?

   A: That Liz doesn't know them well.

9. W: I have an extra ticket to the concert tonight. Would you like to come along?

   M: Thanks, but I already have my own ticket. Perhaps you can sell the other one at the door.

   Q: What does the man suggest?

   A: Trying to sell the ticket.

10. W: I'd like to take a trip to China during my spring vacation. Can you give me any ideas about where to go?

    M: I can tell you about the places I've visited. But I think you'd better get a professional to make your arrangements.

    Q: What advice did the man give to the woman?

    A: See a travel agent.

【李阳·克立兹三最口腔肌肉训练记录为：10秒】

❋ ❋ ❋ ❋ ❋ ❋

　　学习外语不过就是体力劳动，请疯狂地操练你的口腔肌肉，不断突破极限，直至达成完美的国际肌肉！

　　可自己测试时间，也可以与同学朋友进行比赛，非常刺激！

第三章

超级秘诀 一举三得
——口语、听力、发音同时突破！

★ ★ ★ ★ ★ ★ ★ ★ ★ ★ ★

一个一举三得的听力突破法就是直接收集各类试题的听力部分，特别是国外的精彩考题，将其中的地道句子用上面的三个步骤进行处理。这样可以使你大量地接触听力陷阱，反复地熟悉考试小把戏，获得免疫力，达成超越一般听力的超级听力能力，在听力考试中像母语一样"立刻反应、百发百中"，成为考试专家和高手！除此之外，你还有两个特别收获：

1、听力考试里的句子同时又是经过考试专家精心挑选的、绝对地道的语言精华，铺盖面特别广。在大喊听力考试题的同时，口语能力不知不觉地获得长足的进步。听力考试题是最好的口语学习资料！

2、听力考试一般配备磁带，绝大多数的磁带是由美国人朗读的，发音纯正地道，所以通过反复听和模仿这些磁带，你的发音又可以获得改进。

鉴于以上原因，为了帮助大家在短期内突破听力难关，李阳·克立兹工作室为大家准备了这套书：口语突破听力、听力突破口语、口语听力共同辉煌。本套书荟萃了国内外最新的听力资料，并全部总结成实用的口语，包括单句、小对话和长篇对话三个部分，并按照出题者的"阴谋"进行了分类，以便你反复练习，熟能生巧，应付自如。这些分类大致包括：数字；计算；推理；比较；条件；让步；场所；暗示等等。另外，这套书还配备了一套由美国播音员按照"三最"要求朗读的录音带，使你的听力获得超强度、高标准的训练。这套录音带所容纳的内容是一般录音带的数倍。整个专辑总共包含地道口语近三千句(三千笔财富)。精通这套资料，将使你的听力足以应付一切考试，同时口语能力获得大面积提高，能够和英美人士进行自由的双向交流，并为担任口译打下坚实基础。

神 奇 效 果

■ 只要稍微听一听、看一看、读一读这本书，下一次参加考试的时侯，感觉一定会"轻松多了"！

■ 如果将这套书里的句子全部脱口而出，那你的听力将威力无比。

■ 如果明天考试，即使你今天开始临阵磨枪，把这些教材里面的句子大声朗读一遍，明天考试时照样效果不凡！

■ 我们特别聘请发音地道、优美的美国播音员兼演员为大家录制的这套浓缩磁带，一定要充分利用。按照李阳·克立兹理论，一盘磁带就可以彻底突破发音关，那么你也可以用这套听力磁带来彻底改进你的发音，享受说一口纯正英语的自豪。

第 四 章

★
★
★
★
★
★
★
★
★

如何在听不懂的情况下照样选对答案

（中英文对照）

——学一点"害人"的、只对考试有用的技巧！

——三大实用技巧，抓住听力考试题的致命弱点，在紧张的听力考场上运筹帷幄、稳操胜券！

这里所谈的技巧以托福考试为样本，它是英语考试的典范，国内的高考、四级、六级等考试都在逐渐向它靠拢。

以下比较难的部分采取中英文对照形式，其余的只给出英文，所有资料都适合进行三最口腔肌肉训练。编写这个部分的一个疯狂目的是要求大家能够用英文来告诉别人如何对付听力考试！这是李阳·克立兹的一贯信念：一步登天！

首先让我们来熟悉标准听力考试的结构：

[1] The Listening Comprehension section of the TOEFL contains fifty questions. There are three sections to this part of the test.

[2] Part A: In this section you hear a short statement 『陈述；叙述』and you are asked to select the answer closest in meaning to what you heard. There are twenty questions in

Part A.

[3] Part B: In this section you hear a short dialogue between two speakers. A third speaker will then ask you a question about what was said. There are fifteen questions in Part B.

[4] Part C: In this section you hear three longer talks, either a conversation between two people or a lecture given by one person. Each talk is followed by four to six questions, for which you are asked to select the best answer. There are fifteen questions in part C.

[5] Total time for the section is about thirty minutes. There are fifty questions total on this section.

【李阳·克立兹三最口腔肌肉训练记录为:35 秒】

在进行听力考试的时候,你要面对巨大的时间压力! 因为:

You can't take any extra time for hard questions!(对于难的问题,你没有多余的时间!)

无论是听懂还是听不懂,难还是简单,你都只有同样的时间! 只有一次机会! 很多人由于心理素质差和缺乏技巧而在听力考试中一败涂地! 所以听力考试就像一场竞争激烈的体育运动! 有人把它比作打网球:

[1] Even if you've never played tennis, you've probably at some point in your life seen it played. Your goal for this section is to learn to play the game of Listening Comprehension. Understanding what is on the tape is only one small part of the game. First of all, you need to learn to pace 『为…定步调;掌握速度』yourself. Think for a moment about what makes a good tennis player.

[2] Bad tennis players spend a lot of time watching the ball and running to try to catch up to it.

[3] Good tennis players spend a lot of time watching their opponents to anticipate 『预料』where the ball will go so

that they can be there first and be ready to hit it back.

[4] Most people take the Listening Comprehension section the way bad tennis players play tennis——always running a little bit behind. To do well on this section, you need to stay one step ahead of your opponent——you need to stay ahead of the questions.

【李阳·克立兹三最口腔肌肉训练记录为：35秒】

翻译的最高境界：中国人说中国话

（即使你从来没有打过网球，但你可能看过别人打。你现在要做的就是学会玩听力考试的游戏。听懂只是这个游戏的一个小部分。首先，你需要学习如何控制自己的步调。现在让我们来看看一个好的网球运动员是如何做的。

普通的网球运动者把大部分的时间用在盯着别人的球，然后再仓促地跑过去接球，完全处于被动地位；而网球高手则是盯着对手，并预料球的方向以便先发制人。

大多数参加听力考试的人表现得就像那个普通的网球运动者，总是慢一步。所以要想做好听力考试，你必须比对手先行一步，你必须走在问题的前面。）

下面我们来谈一谈技巧。李阳·克立兹听力训练的硬功夫要求是：像母语那样去听懂！这里所谈的技巧主要是帮助那些听力很差的人对付考试、蒙混过关，当然对具有英语真功夫的朋友，这些技巧也会帮助他们更加稳操胜券！

技巧一：*Reading Ahead* 提前阅读

You have about twelve seconds to answer each of the questions in Parts A and B, no matter how hard or easy each question may seem. The best use of these twelve seconds is to use them to get a sense of 『进行大致了解』 the upcoming 『即将到来的』 question. To do this:

Read the answer choices before you hear each question.

（在听每个问题之前，先抓紧时间阅读四个选择答案。）

When you take the test, you will hear the voice on the tape reading the directions for Part A. You will not be able to see the questions for Part A until the directions have been read. However, you should turn the page the instant 『一…就』you hear the end of the directions, which sounds something like this:

Sentence(B) "Could you help me carry these books" is closest in meaning to the sentence you heard. Therefore you should choose answer (B).

As you are turning the page you will hear

Go on to the next page. Now let us begin Part A with question number one.

But by then you should already be reading the answer choices to question 1 in order to get ready to listen. Then, as soon as you hear

Question number one ...

followed by whatever that question may be, choose your answer and mark it as quickly as possible. Now you can use the rest of the twelve seconds to read the answer choices for question 2, and so on.

（听到第一个问题后，就迅速选择答案，然后以最快的速度标记答案。这时你就可以用剩余的/节省出来的十二秒钟去阅读下一个问题的选择答案。）

The key to this method is discipline 『纪律』. You'll find you tend to want to linger 『逗留；耽搁』on each of the questions until you hear the beginning of the next one. DON'T DO IT! That's how you can end up 『以…结果结束』missing two or three questions in a row; if you don't know the answer, GUESS and move on!

（这个方法的关键是纪律。你可能会犹豫不定，在每个问题上耽搁过久，直至你听到下一个问题开始。千万不要这么做！否则你可能会连续错过两、三个问题，如果你不知道答案,只管猜,然后就继续前进。)

【李阳·克立兹三最口腔肌肉训练记录为:60秒】

提前阅读技巧四步骤总结

【请用英语讲给别人听】

* *When you hear the end of the instructions, begin reading the answer choices for question 1.*

* *As soon as you hear the question, guess.*

* *Use the rest of the twelve seconds to read the answer choices for the next question.*

* *Repeat steps 2 and 3 until the end of Part A.*

【李阳·克立兹三最口腔肌肉训练记录为:10秒】

技巧二: *Guess the Topic* 猜测话题

Staying ahead of the questions helps you overcome the problems caused by the time pressure on this section. Any time you don't see the correct answer, just guess and keep moving. Now that you're keeping up with the ball in this game, that is, staying ahead of the questions, you can begin to practice the second skill you need to win — anticipating 『预料』what your opponent will do. It's time to tackle 『处理;应付』the second major difficulty of this section.

(走在问题的前面帮助你克服了由于时间紧张而引起的问题。如果你一下找不到正确的答案,就只管进行猜测,然后继续做下面的题目。既然你已经能够跟得上这场听力游戏中"球"的速度,那么你就可以开始操练第二个技巧——预料你对手的举动。现在是对付第二个主要难题的时候了。)

22

【李阳·克立兹三最口腔肌肉训练记录为:15秒】

1、No Context 没有上下文/没有前后关联

In face-to-face conversation there are a lot of things that you rely on to help you understand what the other person is saying——facial expressions, hand gestures, and what you know about the person or the topic all give additional meaning to the words used. Furthermore if this person uses some words or expressions that you're not familiar with, you can use the context of the rest of the conversation to help you figure out what they mean.

（在面对面的谈话中，你可以依靠很多东西来帮助你理解对方的话——面部表情、手势和你所了解的对方的情况和话题，这些都给你额外的含义。另外，如果对方用了你不熟悉的单词和表达法，你可以借助其余对话的线索来理解它们的含义。）

All of these cues 『线索；提示』are gone on parts A and B of the Listening Comprehension section. Aside from time, the largest hurdle to get over in order to do well on this section is that lack of context. For the questions on Parts A and B the information presented is isolated『孤立的』. The question you're waiting to hear on the tape could be about anything. You can't see the person speaking, so it's much harder to figure out their emotional state or opinion.

（在听力第一和第二部分，这些线索通通消失。除了时间的因素，这个部分的最大障碍就是缺乏上下文，所有的信息都是孤立的。你准备听到的可能是任何东西。你看不到那个人在说话，所以理解他们的感情状态和想法非常困难。）

【李阳·克立兹三最口腔肌肉训练记录为：30秒】

2、Guess the Topic 猜测话题

You're reading ahead, you've heard the end of the instructions for Part A, and you begin to read the answer choices for question 1. Let's say the choices are:

1.（A）I never heard the lecture.

（B）That kind of lecture never fascinates me.

（C）That lecture was the most fascinating I've heard.

（D）I would have preferred a different lecture.

What are most of the answer choices about? A lecture. So the stem will have to be about the same thing. Now you have a context. You know it will have something to do with a lecture. Your task is to find out more information about it.

【李阳·克立兹三最口腔肌肉训练记录为：23秒】

技巧三：*Three Ways to Find the Right Answer*
三个找到正确答案的方法

Reading ahead helps you keep up. Guessing the topic supplies you with a context and helps you listen actively. These three techniques help you narrow down『缩小；限制范围』your choices whether or not you have actually under-stood what is spoken on the tape.

【李阳·克立兹三最口腔肌肉训练记录为：8秒】

1. OPPOSITES 相反的选择

One of ETS's『美国教育考试机构』favorite kind of wrong answers is one that traps people who almost under-stood the stem. It looks pretty similar to the correct answer, but means the opposite.

For example：

（A）Sunday is a day Mary often works.

（B）Mary rarely works on Sunday.

（C）Some days Mary's work is awful.

(D) Mary has had a terrible cough since Sunday.

In the example above, (A) and (B) are what we call opposites, that is, both statements could not be true. Of a typical Listening Comprehension section, one third to one half of the questions contain opposites. This is good news for you because:

If there is one pair of opposites in the answer choices, one of them is the right answer!

（如果在四个选择答案中有两个对立/相反的句子，那么其中一个就是正确答案。）

Even if you never hear the question, you now have a 50 percent chance of answering this question correctly. Furthermore a pair of opposites in the answer choices tells you exactly what the stem will be about. You only have to listen to hear confirmation『确认；证实』of one or the other of the two opposites.

Find the opposites in the example below:

1. (A) Stone does not enjoy clothes shopping.
   (B) Stone ate while he tried on the clothes.
   (C) Buying clothing is a pleasure for Stone.
   (D) Not one piece of clothing was available in his size.

In this example, the opposites are (A), which says that Stone doesn't like to buy clothes, and (C), which says that he does. Now when you hear the stem, you only need to find out which one is true. The stem is:

If there's one thing Stone hates, it's buying clothes.

so the correct answer is (A).

Now try this one. First, read the answer choices and

find the opposites.

    2.（A）I think your desk is far too tiny.

      （B）Your desk is too messy.

      （C）I think you need a new desk.

      （D）I cleaned up your desk.

The opposites are（B）and（D）. If you didn't recognize them, you need to be a little more broad in your understanding of the term.（B）implies that the desk is messy, and（D）implies that the desk is clean. That's enough for them to be considered opposites. So now all you need to do is decide if the desk is clean or messy. When you hear the stem

My, your desk could sure use some tidying up!

you know the answer is（B）.

2. COMMON SENSE 常识

The people who write the TOEFL have very conservative tastes. None of their statements or dialogues will contain anything controversial, violent, passionate, or silly.

（编写托福考试的人比较保守，他们的句子和对话都不会包含有争议的、激烈的、热烈的和愚蠢的东西。）

Remember, you can use common sense to eliminate『除去；排除』three types of wrong answers:

Type 1: Answer choices that are too extreme『极端』.

    （A）Sunday is a day Mary often works.

    （B）Mary rarely works on Sunday.

    （C）Some days Mary's work is awful.

    （D）Mary has had a terrible cough since Sunday.

Answer（C）is too extreme to be a good bet. ETS

would probably say someone's work was "unsatisfactory" or even "bad," but not "awful." Just remember, ETS can't afford to offend anyone: any answers that might be controversial are automatically wrong.

Type 2: Answer choices that have the wrong subject, for example:

(A) He is a good football player.

(B) He doesn't understand football at all.

(C) He lives right across that field.

(D) Playing football indoors is forbidden.

Since most of the answer choices are about football, you know that "football" is the topic of the stem, therefore you can eliminate answer (C). Now here's the stem

He sure seems right at home on the football field.

The closest in meaning is answer (A). By the way, did you notice that (A) and (B) were opposites?

Type 3: Answer choices that are just plain silly 『明显的愚蠢』, for example:

(A) Rob is too tall to be an actor.

(B) Rob's performance was excellent.

(C) He didn't see Rob on stage.

(D) Rob was suspended above the stage.

Answer (A) is just silly. How can someone be too tall to be an actor? Answer choice (D) is weird 『奇怪的』too. Now here's the stem.

27

W: How was Rob in the new play last night?

M: Great! He was head and shoulders above the rest of the cast.

Q: What does the man mean?

The expression "head and shoulders above" means "far better than," so the closest in meaning is answer (B). Notice that both silly answers, (A) and (D), are based on literal interpretations『字面理解』of the expression "head and shoulders above." If you hear something in the stem that doesn't make literal sense, it's an idiom. Idioms are a signal to be on the lookout for『提防；寻找』answer choices that take that idiom literally and turn it into something silly.

3. SOUND-ALIKES 同音同声词

Another of ETS's favorite trap answers is what we call a sound-alike. Sound-alikes take some of the words and sounds from the statement or dialogue and rearrange them so that they have a totally different meaning. Remember this example?

> (A) *Sunday is a day Mary often works.*
> (B) *Mary rarely works on Sunday.*
> (C) *Some days Mary's work is awful.*
> (D) *Mary has had a terrible cough since Sunday.*

The statement was

Sunday is usually Mary's day off.

We already found the opposites in these answers, (A) and (B), and one extreme answer, (C). So now look at how ETS might trap you with sounds. Notice how many things in the answer choices echo『回响』the word "off" in the statement——"often", "awful", and "cough". And in answer （C）, the one answer choice without Sunday, has been replaced with "Some days" . The right answer, （B）, is one of the pair of opposites, is not silly or extreme, and contains the fewest sound-alikes.

After you've found the opposites and silly answers, choose the answer choice that sounds "least" like what you heard on the tape.

You'll notice that many sound-alikes can also be eliminated using common sense.

Summary of Strategy
技 巧 总 结

Step 1: *Read the answer choices before you hear the question.*

Step 2: *While reading, look for*
   * *The topic for Part A.*
   * *The topic or the question for Part B.*
   * *Opposite pairs in the answer choices*
   * *Anything that violates common sense.*

Step 3: *Listen to confirm what you found in Step 2.*

Step 4: *Choose your answer. If you are still undecided, choose the answer choice containing the fewest sounds from the statement or dialogue.*

【李阳·克立兹三最口腔肌肉训练记录为：15秒】

第五章

听力突破小怪招

（中英文对照）

——请同时用中英文像国际专家一样讲给别人听！

★ ★ ★ ★ ★ ★ ★ ★ ★ ★ ★

Many people who have taken the TOEFL have reported that the tape was very difficult to hear, either because the volume was too low or because the quality of the tape player was very bad. Therefore you can't count on being able to hear the tape clearly. While you are preparing to take the TOEFL, there are some things you can practice to help you acquire the skills to better understand what you'll eventually be hearing on the tape.

*   ***Talk on the phone (in English of course).***

*   ***Listen to talk shows and news reports on the radio.***

*   ***Practice English where it's really hard to hear. If you have people with whom you can practice speaking English, try to go to noisy places to do it, such as restaurants or nightclubs or even train stations. If you can (even if it feels silly), try talking to each other without looking at each other, so you don't have the opportunity to use facial expressions or gestures to give you clues as to what your conversation partner is saying.***

（到嘈杂的地方去操练英语，比如说餐馆或是夜总会，甚至火车站这样的地方。虽然感觉有点傻，但如果可能的话，试一试在不看对方的情况下进行谈话，这样你就没有机会借助面部表情或动作的线索来理解对方的意思。）

【李阳·克立兹三最口腔肌肉训练记录为：40秒】

第 六 章

英语听力分类轰炸

——配备大量精彩实例！

——请赶紧用"三最"法将这些财富彻底据为己有！

——口语能力和听力能力都将同时获得大幅提升！

★ ★ ★ ★ ★ ★ ★ ★ ★ ★ ★

　　我们只是大致地分几个主要类型，而不去进行彻底的、严格的、系统的分类，这样又会走入误区，把大部分时间耗费在理解这些分类上！只要想想我们的母语！我们在脱口而出的时候，并不知道这个句子是比较句还是因果状语从句，但是完美地完成了交流任务，这也是我们学习英语最终的境界！

　　最最重要的是张大你的嘴，刻苦操练，疯狂地脱口而出每一个句子，建立深厚的感情！

疯 狂 开 始

　　在录音带上，前五十句比较慢速，请大家自己查阅字典将发音标记在单词旁边，然后仔细听并大声模仿美国老师的发音。五十句以后的成百上千句，我们将采用"三最"标准，强化你的听力和口腔肌肉，训练超级英语硬功夫和实战能力。

31

第一节:英语单句的七种主要类型

第一部分:对数字的敏感

【短评】数字是看起来最简单,但最难听懂和脱口而出的奇怪东西! 我在上大学的时候,有专门对数字的听力训练,但效率非常低。一个简便而有效的方法就是收集包含数字的句子,然后用三步法进行疯狂操练,再和同学合作,进行汉翻英、英翻汉快速数字口译训练。这样,数字很快就成为你的朋友!

1. John will be thirty on November fourteenth.

= On November fourteenth John will celebrate his day.

【几乎没有人能够讲对!】

2. Since your suitcase weighs <u>sixty</u> pounds, you'll have to pay <u>overweight</u>.

= The wight of the suitcase is sixty pounds.

3. The International Office has moved to 70 South Speedway.

= The new address of the International Office is 70 South Speedway.

4. Forty students will receive their Ph. D. degrees in

industrial engineering this semester.

= A doctoral 『博士的』 degree will be awarded 『授予』to forty students this semester.

5. *A one-way ticket 『单程票』 to Washington costs eighty dollars.*

= Eighty dollars is the price of a ticket to Washington.

6. *You have fifteen minutes to finish this section of the test.*

= There are fifteen minutes left for this section of the test.

7. *Jane lives in room fourteen on the first floor of Parks Tower.*

= Room fourteen is Jane's.

8. *It only costs fifteen cents to call Miami after five o'-clock.*

= After five o'clock a call to Miami costs fifteen cents.

9. *All of the English classes will meet in room 170 this semester.*

= English classes will all meet in room 170 this semester.

【注】**meet**: vi. 集会;开会;会合;见面;(会议等)召开。

* Let's meet together again tomorrow.
* We must meet again to discuss it.
* The student council meets next week.
  (学生自治会下周要开会。)

33

10. *Turn to page 16 in your textbooks, and do the first fifteen problems.* = The problems on page 16 are assigned 『分配;指定』.

11. Today's low temperature was thirty degrees.

= Thirty degrees was today's low temperature 『最低温度』.

12. I need eighteen xerox copies 『复印件』 before my eight o'clock meeting tomorrow morning.

= At eight o'clock tomorrow morning I will need eighteen copies.

13. The rate of exchange is thirteen-to-one.

= Thirteen-to-one is the rate of exchange『货币兑换率』.

14. I-90 is one of the busiest interstate highways 『州际公路』 in the nation. = I-90 is a busy highway.

【联想】当我看到这个句子的时候，我的脑海中就会出现这个的画面：我陪同外国客人到一个城市去进行投资情况调查，结果路上发生了大堵车，于是我就脱口而出：

This is one of the busiest intercity highways in the province.

（这是本省最繁忙的市际公路之一。）

15. CBS news is on channel Thirteen at six o'clock.

= Channel Thirteen carries CBS news.

16. The answers may be found on page 90 in your textbook. = Page 90 has the answers on it.

17. You need an eighteen-cent stamp for this package.

= It will cost eighteen cents to mail the package.

18. Flight forty to Dallas is now boarding at gate two.

= The flight now boarding is number forty.

19. *Fifteen percent of the students who took the examination scored above 450.*

= A score of 450 or more was achieved by 15 percent of the students tested.

20. *W: Prices are really going up. I had to pay three dollars for a shirt yesterday, and I used to pay only two.*

M: *I know what you mean【口语要素】. My sweaters cost me over ten now.*

Q: *How much do shirts cost now?*

A: *3 dollars each.*

Audi 100

第二部分:听力小把戏——计算

【短评】这个部分比较能够测试一个人英语的真功夫,因为必须几乎全部听懂才有可能选择对答案,而且有些计算即使是母语,也不一定能立刻算对。但这并不可怕,听力计算题的小把戏是有限的,在疯狂三步曲的轰炸下,这些都是小菜一碟!

1. *Stone bought a used book for ＄6, saving about ＄2.50.*

= A new book costs ＄8.50.

2. *Sandy bought a 200-dollar camera for 165 dollars.*

= Sandy paid 35 dollars less than the regular price for

the camera.

【注】这是一个高级精品句，因为用了一般学习者最难掌握的比较句型。

3. City College had 520 students in 1960, but since then, the school has doubled its enrollment 『登记/注册人数』.

= In 1960 City College had 520 students.

4. Miss Smith always gets to the store a half-hour early in order to check the register 『登记本；收银机』 **before the store opens at ten o'clock.**

= Miss Smith arrives at 9:30 A.M.【高级精品长句】

5. By the time I pay 250 dollars for my rent, I only have half of my salary left.【听力典型难题】

= The speaker's salary is 500 dollars.

【很多"下海"的人都有此同感】

6. Their flight was scheduled to depart 『离开；起程』 **at noon, but the plane was delayed for half an hour.**

= The plane left at 12:30 P.M.

【注】我们在这里稍微休息一下，来彻底掌握这个 **schedule** 王牌单词。

schedule：安排时间；列入时间表。**scheduled**：过去分词"退化"成形容词，表示"预定的；排定的；严格按照时间表进行的"。

＊ The meeting is scheduled on Friday.

（会议安排在星期五。）

＊ The plane is scheduled to take off at 4.

（飞机定于四时起飞。）

＊ The president is scheduled to make a speech tomorrow.【高级精品长句】

（总统定于明天发表讲话。）

        ★ The new highway is scheduled for completion by
           the end of the year. (新公路定于年内竣工。)

**7. The stadium seats 『可容纳』 about 50, 000 people,
but it was half empty for last night's game.**

   = 25,000 people attended last night's game.

**8. Dr. Jones got to the corner at 8: 40 A.M., missing
the bus by five minutes.**【听力典型难题】

   = The bus left at 8:35 A.M.

**9. If Jane can type forty words a minute, Judy can
probably type eighty.**

   = Jane types half as fast as Judy.

   (简打字速度是朱迪的一半。)【高级精品句】

**10. These end tables 『茶几』 are on sale for $ 85 each
or $ 150 for a pair.**

   = One end table costs $ 85.

**11. The class begins at eight o'clock, but Bill is always
fifteen minutes late.**

   = Bill gets to class at eight-fifteen.

**12. We expected『预期；预料；打算』to sell forty tickets,
but we sold twice as many.**

   = We sold eighty tickets.

**13. Since the taxi was late, Dr. Jones didn't get to the
airport until eleven o'clock, missing his flight by
half an hour.**

   = Dr. Jones's plane left at 10:30.

   【注】 这是一个高级精品句，因为里面用到了
   "**not...until**"这个王牌结构。

14. **Mr. Black has to leave his house at 8: 30 in order to get to work by 9: 00.**

   = Mr. Black must spend a half-hour driving to work.

   【注】在这里再次提醒大家一定要注意"私有化"，请反复大喊直至自豪地说出：

   * I have to leave my house at 8: 30 in order to get to work by 9:00.

15. **Alice was <u>shortchanged</u>『少找钱给（某人）』 ten dollars when the <u>teller</u>『（银行）出纳员』 cashed『兑现』 her $ 300 check.**

   = Alice was ten dollars short.

16. **My <u>watch says</u> 9: 30, but I always <u>set it ten minutes ahead</u>.**

   （我总是调快十分钟。)【一个好主意】

   = The time is 9:20.

17. **This recipe『食谱』 will only <u>serve</u> ten people, and we expect『期待；预期』 at least twenty.**

   = We should make a double recipe.

18. **Since the <u>shuttle bus</u>『穿梭车；短距离往返的公车』 only goes halfway from State University to married student housing『住宅』, Bob and Carole have to walk half a mile to the bus stop.**

   = Bob and Carole live one mile from State University in married student housing.【听力计算难题】

19. **John was supposed to arrive in time for the noon meal, but he was two hours late.**

   = John arrived at two o'clock.

20. At the end of the season, many of these six-ty-dollar dresses will be on sale【出售】for half price.

= The dresses will cost 30 dollars.

【再次提醒】你成功的喜悦不是来自把数字算对了！这不是学习语言的目的！你必须将每一句话像母语一样脱口而出。

* M: I ran all the way to the bus stop, but the man at the ticket counter told me the bus left 5 minutes ago. (我老远跑到车站，但是售票亭里的人告诉我，巴士已在五分钟前开走了。)

W: That's too bad. Those buses leave only every 50 minutes.

(这真糟糕，那种巴士每五十分钟只有一班。)

Q: How long does the man have to wait?

A: 45 minutes.

BMW 5-Series

第三部分:相关

【短评】这类考题一般包含两个或两个以上的人，他们之间有着某种关系。很多英语学习者存在这样一个问题：句子中出现了自己不熟悉的名字而误以为是一个新单词；或是出现了两个以上的名字而导致混乱。当然，解答这类题有一些猜测的技巧，但最好的技巧还是像母语一样完全听懂！

1. *Alice wants to transfer* 『转学；调动』 *to Beijing University because she has many friends studying there.* = Alice plans to study at Beijing University with her friends.

2. *Sally borrowed her sister's bicycle.*

= Sally's sister lent her a bicycle.【像绕口令一样疯狂反复操练】

3. *Ann would like us to pick her up* 『（用车）接；搭载』 *at the bus station.*

= Ann wants us to meet 『迎接；遇到；碰见』 her.

【注】顺便送给大家一些财富：

* I went to meet my father at the station.

（我去车站迎接我父亲。）

* You will be met at the station by my wife.

（我太太会在火车站迎接你们。）

* I met many new words in the book.

（我在那本书上碰见许多新词。）

4. *Bill bought his wife a suit for their anniversary* 『周年纪念』.

= He bought her a suit.

5. *I don't remember the last name of Stone's teacher.*

= The speaker does not remember the teacher's last name.

6. *Pat refused to accept John's invitation to the party.*

= Pat did not go to the party.

7. *Nancy made Paul the knit scarf* 『围巾』 *he has on.*

= Paul has a knit 『编织的』 scarf.【简单但很难听懂】

8. **Tom sent his roommate a card to wish him a happy birthday.**

   = Tom wished his roommate a happy birthday.

9. **Bill's sister was very proud when he graduated.**

   = When Bill graduated, his sister was very proud of him.

10. **James's mother had already gone to work when he got home.**

    = James's mother was at work when he got home.

11. **Last night at the party we finally met Mary's Uncle Charles.** = Last night we were introduced to Charles, Mary's uncle.

    [ˈkrɪtəˌsaɪz]

12. **Bob resented** 『憎恨；厌恶』 **his father's criticizing the plans for his new office building.**

    = Bob was unhappy when his father criticized his plans for a new office building.

13. **Mrs. Williams asked her lawyer to draw up** 『草拟；起草』 **a will naming her grandson as the sole** 『唯一的』 **beneficiary** 『受益人』.

    = The lawyer wrote the will 『遗嘱；遗书』 for Mrs. Williams.

14. **Larry took his brother's car to the car wash** 『洗汽车的场地或营业所』. = Larry washed his brother's car.

15. **Paul wants his wife to go back to school next semester** 『一学期；半学年』.

    = Paul would like his wife to finish her education.

41

16. Mrs. Martin told Dr. Smith's secretary to cancel『取消』**her appointment.**

= Mrs. Martin could not keep her appointment with Dr. Smith.

17. Jeff's family was happy when he married Nancy.

（当杰夫和南希结婚的时候，杰夫的家人非常高兴。）

= Jeff's family approved of his marrying Nancy.【高级精品句】

18. Professor Baker asked his graduate『研究所的』**assistant**『助手；助教』**to give the lecture today.**

= Professor Baker's graduate assistant was asked to give today's lecture.

19. Mary refused to return Bill's telephone call.

= Mary did not telephone Bill.

20. Mr. Johnson wants his nephew『侄子』**to go into business with him because he doesn't have a son of his own.**

（强生先生希望他的侄子和他一起做生意，因为他自己没有儿子。）

= Mr. Johnson hopes that he and his nephew will go into business together.

Classic

第四部分:特殊句型——否定

【短评】这里面的所有句子都是"高级精品句"，这里面的所有句子都是英语学习的难点，能脱口而出一句就可以自豪一个星期！亲爱的朋友，看到这么多财富，应该感到无比激动和兴奋！吃掉它们！消化它们！疯狂起来吧！

1. **_The students had never seen so much snow before._**
   （学生们从没见过这么大的雪。）【南方学生有同感】
   = This was the first time that the students had seen such a lot of snow.

2. **_We have no students who are not insured._**
   = All students have insurance『保险』.

3. **_John could hardly eat his dessert『餐后甜点』._**
   = He ate the dessert with difficulty.
   【注】"hardly"是一个中国英语学习者认得但几乎从来不用的高级副词：
   * I could hardly believe it.（我几乎无法相信它。）
   * His success is hardly possible.
     （他的成功几乎是不可能的。）
   * It is hardly true.（这几乎不可能是真的。）

4. **_The tour was worth neither the time nor the money._**
   （这次旅行既浪费时间又浪费金钱。）【听力大陷阱】
   = The tour was not worth the time or the money.
   【注】我们在这里再次强调一下李阳·克立兹的"不懂只是一次不懂、糊涂只是一次糊涂"原则，真正地和 **"neither...nor"** 建立脱口而出的关系。
   * He neither drinks nor smokes.
     （他既不喝酒也不抽烟。）
   * I like neither coffee nor tea.
     （我既不喜欢咖啡也不喜欢茶。）

43

5. **_Not many brothers are as nice to their sisters as Tom_**

is.

（没有多少人对待姐妹会像汤姆那么好。）【高级精品句】

= Tom is nicer to his sister than most brothers are to their sisters.

6. *She has hardly any friends.*【六星级高级精品句】

= She does not have many friends.

【注】再送给大家一些财富：

* I could hardly wait to hear the news.

（我迫不急待地想听新闻。）

* I was so angry that I could hardly speak.

（我气得几乎说不出话来。）

* I hardly ever （= almost never) go out these days.（这些日子我几乎没有出门。）

7. *There is no better place to practice driving than the shopping center.*

（再也没有比购物中心更适合练习驾驶的地方了。）

= The shopping center is the best place to practice driving.

8. *Nancy likes nothing better than to sleep late.*

（南希最喜欢睡懒觉。）

= Nancy likes to sleep late.

9. *It's not like Mary to be unfriendly, so she must not have seen you when you waved.*

（玛丽可是非常友好的/不友善可不是玛丽的风格！她一定是没有看见你挥手。）

= Mary did not wave 『挥手示意』because she did not see you.

10. *The problem was not uncommon for a young man away from home.*【否定之否定；听力之陷阱】

15. *Their new apartment was no more comfortable than the first one had been.* = Neither the first apartment nor the new one was comfortable.

【注】大家学习到这里的时候，应该停下来和"**no more...than**"建立一下感情，这个短语对于大多数人来说，读懂都不容易，更不用说听懂了。

no more...than: 跟…一样不; 强/好不了多少

* I am no more mad than you are.

（我跟你一样没有发疯。）

not more...than: 不像…那样; 不比…更加

* This question is not more difficult than that one. (这个问题不比那个难。)

16. *There is no harder course than English 190.*

（再也没有比英语 190 更难的课程了。）

= English 190 is the most difficult course.

17. *Betty didn't have to work overtime 『加班』.*

= Betty is not required to work extra hours.

18. *He has never been unfair with his students.*

（他从来没有对学生不公平过。）

= He is always fair.

19. *I can't possibly afford a new car right now.*

= I do not have enough money for a car.

【注】我们在平时说英语时，应注意多使用像"**possibly**"这样的高级副词，那么在听英语时，就不会被这些副词所迷惑了。

* She may possibly come. (她或许会来。)

* I can't possibly do this.

（我实在无法做这件事。）

20. *Business has never been slower 『(商业)不景气的』.*

= The problem was common for young men.

【注】我想很多人都可以马上猜出"**uncommon**"的意思，这是一个前缀"**un**"加上"**common**"组成的。虽然你能猜出这个单词的意思，但按照李阳·克立兹的标准，你根本没有掌握这个单词！再次呼吁：学习语言不要太多理智的分析！要感情！要脱口而出的真功夫！

* an uncommon experience（不寻常的经历）

* an uncommon ability（非凡的才能）

11. *Professor Kemp speaks neither Japanese nor Chinese.*

= Professor Kemp does not speak Japanese and Chinese.

【注】这个句型是我们刚刚讲过的，大家非常熟悉的句型！但可惜的是，这么多年来，我几乎没有听到过有人能脱口而出这个句型！这里再送给大家几个类似的实用句子：

* Neither my father nor I were there.

* She is neither in the kitchen nor in the living room.（她既不在厨房也不在客厅。）

12. *Jane's family hasn't ever met her friend, Bob.*

（简的家人还没有见过她的朋友鲍伯。）

= Bob and Jane's family have never met.

13. *There isn't any doubt about it.*

（毫无疑问。）【高级口语要素】

= There is no doubt.

45

14. *That copy machine is absolutely* 『绝对地；完全地』 *useless.*

= The machine cannot be used.

（生意从来没有这么不景气过。）

= Business was better before.

Classic

第五部分：令人迷惑的比较

【短评】在我的记忆中，到目前为止，我还没有见到过完全正确使用和脱口而出"比较句"的人，我自己也是在广东电台工作的时候，才专门自我培训过这方面的能力。现在，我为大家收集了二十个经典比较句，供你集中轰炸！脱口而出比较句是高级口语能力的一个特征。从今天开始拥有这个能力吧！

1. ***We haven't lived here as long as the Smiths have.***

    = The Smiths have lived here longer than we have.

2. ***Betty prefers living at home with her parents to renting her own apartment.***

    = Betty likes living at home.

3. ***When the new students have been here a little longer, I'm sure that they will feel less homesick*『思乡的；想家的』*.***

    = The new students have not been here very long.

4. ***Kathy is better looking than her roommate, Ann.***

    = Kathy is prettier than Ann.

5. ***The University is farther away than I thought.***

    （大学比我想像的/原来以为的要远。）【高级精品句】

47

= The University is not as near as I thought.

6. *Bill gets less exercise than he should.*

（最好的翻译方法是：比尔应该加强锻炼。）

= Bill should exercise more.

7. *Ellen isn't a bit* 『一点也不』 *like her husband, Tom.*

= Ellen and Tom are very different.

8. *Ann prefers cold weather to hot weather.*

= Ann likes cold weather better than hot weather.

9. *Traditionally the most successful small business in the United States is the restaurant business.*

= There are more successful restaurants in the United States than any other small business.

【李阳·克立兹三最口腔肌肉训练记录为：6秒】

10. *Aspirin* 『阿斯匹林』 *is as good as anything for colds and flu.* = One of the best remedies 『药物』 for colds and flu is aspirin.

【注】(as) ... as anything：非常；无比。

　　＊It's (as) easy as anything.【王牌精品句】

　　　（这非常简单。）

11. *Writing this term paper was a bigger job than I thought it would be.*

（写这个学期论文比我想像的难多了。）【高级精品句】

= Writing this term paper 『论文；报告』 is not as easy as I thought it would be.

【李阳·克立兹三最口腔肌肉训练记录为：4秒】

12. *She has been able to learn English more quickly than I had imagined.*

（她学习英语的速度比我想像的要快。）

= I imagined that she would learn English more slowly than she did.

【李阳·克立兹三最口腔肌肉训练记录为：4秒】

13. *Some people think that jogging* 『慢跑』*is better for your health, but in my opinion, playing tennis is more fun.*

= I like to play tennis more than I like to jog.

【李阳·克立兹三最口腔肌肉训练记录为：5秒】

14. *Jeff was no more surprised than I was when Tom moved out of the dorm.* = Neither Jeff nor I was surprised.【高级精品句；听力难点】

（杰夫和我都不感到惊讶。）

【注】我们再来熟悉一下一个比较难建立感情的结构：

no more … than。

no more … than：和…同样不

　　＊ He can no more speak Chinese than I can.

　　　（他和我一样不会说中文。）

15. *According to government statistics, the older one is when he gets married, the less likely* 『可能发生的』*it is that he'll get a divorce.*【绝对实用】

= People who get married young have a greater probability of getting a divorce.

（结婚早的人离婚的可能性大。）

【李阳·克立兹三最口腔肌肉训练记录为：6秒】

16. *A steak dinner costs ten dollars at most restaurants, but only three dollars at City Steak House.*

= A steak dinner at City Steak House is cheaper than at most restaurants.

49

【李阳·克立兹三最口腔肌肉训练记录为:6秒】

17. John studies harder than Bill, but for some reason Bill gets better grades『成绩;分数』on the exams.

= Bill does not study as hard as John.

18. Larry's son doesn't look like him at all.

= Larry and his son look very different.

19. We had more than enough time to get there.

= There was plenty of time to get there.

（时间非常充裕。）

20. Mrs. Smith hasn't traveled nearly as much as her husband has.

= Mrs. Smith has traveled less than her husband has.

【李阳·克立兹三最口腔肌肉训练记录为:5秒】

Ferrari 456 GT

第六部分:条件句和虚拟语气

【短评】按照李阳·克立兹理论,通过对一句话的脱口而出,牢固地掌握一条语法。当我们谈到条件句和虚拟语气时,我就送给大家两句话:

* If you work hard, you are bound to succeed.

（如果你努力工作的话,你肯定会成功。）

* If he hadn't lived among the workers for so many years, he wouldn't have been able to write such a good novel.

（假如他没有和工人一起生活这么多年,他不可能写出这么好的小说。）

第二句有些人会觉得有些过时，但无论从内容上，还是语法结构上，它都是一个好句子！

下面为大家提供了二十个这样的句子，而且都是出考试题目的人精心挑选出来的，更加具有代表性，是英语的精华和难点。请再次疯狂起来！

1. **If you are ready we can go to the party together.**

   = You and I will be able to go to the party as soon as you are ready.

   【注】为了加深印象，请脱口而出下面这个句子：

   * Will you tell him as soon as he gets back.

   （他一回来你就告诉他好吗？）

2. **Mary could have gotten better grades if she had studied more.**

   （如果玛丽再刻苦一点，她会取得更好的成绩。）

   【高级精品句】

   = Mary did not get better grades because she did not study.

3. **The project would have been approved**『批准；赞成』 **if it hadn't been for the budget**『预算』.

   （如果不是预算的原因，这个项目是会被批准的。）

   = The project was not approved because the budget was high『高的』.

   【李阳·克立兹三最口腔肌肉训练记录为：4秒】

4. **If we had needed to get in touch with them, we could have sent a telegram.**

   （如果我们当时需要和他们联系，我们会发电报的。）

   = We did not send a telegram because we did not need to get in touch with them.

   【李阳·克立兹三最口腔肌肉训练记录为：5秒】

5. **If you usually take a size six, you'll need a size seven in this style.**（如果你平时购买六号的，那么这种式样你就需要七号的。）

= This style runs a little smaller than usual.

6. **If we had arrived on time, we would have gotten good seats.**

（如果那次我们准时到达，我们就会得到好的座位。）

= We did not get good seats because we were late.

【李阳·克立兹三最口腔肌肉训练记录为：4秒】

7. **If he had asked her, she would have gone with him.**

（如果他主动向她提出邀请，她是会和他一起去的。）

= She did not go with him because he did not ask her.

8. **A fur coat like this will last for years if it's cared for properly.**

（一件像这样的毛皮大衣，如果妥善保管，可以穿很多年。）

= Fur coats should be cared for properly to last.

9. **Getting up early isn't difficult if you have an alarm clock.** = It is easier to get up early if you have an alarm clock.

10. **We would have had a better class if Mr. Williams had taught it.**

（如果是威廉姆先生上课，那节课程会更有趣。）

= We were sorry『遗憾』that Mr. Williams didn't teach the class.

11. **If she waits much longer to call a cab, she's going to miss the bus.** = She will miss the bus unless she

calls a cab 『出租汽车』soon.

12. *If you are at the corner by six o'clock, I'll pick you up and take you home.*

= I will meet you at the corner at six o'clock to give you a ride 『乘坐；搭载』home.

13. *Living in another culture isn't difficult if you have the right attitude* 『态度；看法』*.* = A good attitude makes it easy to live in another culture.

【李阳·克立兹三最口腔肌肉训练记录为：4秒】

14. *If Stone keeps studying like he has been, he's going to make himself sick.*

（如果世通继续这么卖命地学习，他会生病的。）

= Stone will get sick from studying so much.

15. *If John had his way* 『为所欲为』*, he would spend all of his time playing tennis.*

（如果让约翰由着性子来，他会把所有的时间都用来打网球的。）

= John wants to play tennis often.

16. *We would have been here sooner if we hadn't gotten lost.*

（如果我们没有迷路的话，我们会早一点到达的。）【高级精品句】

= We were not here sooner because we got lost.

17. *Your order* 『订购的货物』 *will arrive on Saturday if placed by Wednesday.*

= Orders that are placed 『开出（订单）；订货』on Wednesday should arrive on Saturday.

18. **If you want to see the director, he has time this afternoon at two o'clock.**

    = Two o'clock this afternoon is a good time to make an
    appointment with the director 『局长；主任；董事等
    等』.

    【李阳·克立兹三最口腔肌肉训练记录为：5秒】

19. **John would have helped us if he hadn't had such a
bad cold.**

    （如果约翰不是得了重感冒，他会来帮助我们的。）

    = John did not help us because of his cold.

    【李阳·克立兹三最口腔肌肉训练记录为：4秒】

20. **If you had asked the secretary, she would have told
you.**

    （如果你当时问了秘书，她会告诉你的。）

    = The secretary did not tell you because you did not
    ask her.

    【李阳·克立兹三最口腔肌肉训练记录为：4秒】

    最后再送给大家一句典型的虚拟语气句子：

    * **I should have died of hunger if the Communist Party
have not come in1949.** （要是一九四九年共产党不来的话，我
是会饿死的。）

Ferrari Testarossa

第七部分：转折

【短评】在这样的题目中，前后两个句子的意思是相反的，而
且一般是考你后半部分的内容。这类题目出现频率

非常高,但不用担心,下面为大家准备了四十个这样的"实战"试题,包含了所有此类题目的可能出现形式!你现在唯一需要担心的是:如何把它们通通吃掉并消化掉?但区区四十句话对于刻苦和智慧的你来说,真是"小菜一碟"。

1. *I was going to write you a letter, but I decided to call you instead.*

= I called you.

【注】在这里让我们培养一下和"**instead**"的感情。

  * He was sick so his son came instead.

  * She never studies. Instead, she plays tennis all day.

2. *Thank you for inviting us, but I don't believe that we will be able to make* 『(口语)成功;做到;及时赶到』 *it.*

【王牌精品句】

= We could not go to the party.

3. *The hat isn't mine but the coat is.*

【越是简单的句子越难听懂】

= Only the coat is mine.

4. *The State University team usually wins all of its games, but this year it lost two of them.*

= This year the State University team did not win as many games as usual.【高级精品句】

(今年,州立大学队没有像往常赢得那么多。)

5. *Jane usually comes to the ALI to meet her tutor* 『家庭教师;辅导员』*, but Monday she was absent.*

= Jane missed tutoring 『个别指导』on Monday.

6. *Mike was planning to go to graduate school, but he*

didn't have enough money.

= Although Mike had planned to go to graduate school 『研究所/院』, he could not go.

7. ***Mrs. Baker was told that her illness was incurable*** 『不能治疗的』***, but she never gave up.***【王牌精品句】

= Mrs. Baker kept hoping that she would be cured.

8. ***She doesn't like the dorm, but she does like her roommate.***

= She likes her roommate, but not the dorm『学生宿舍』.

9. ***The office is usually closed on Saturdays, but this week the secretary will be there until noon.***

= This week the secretary will be at the office until twelve o'clock Saturday.

【李阳·克立兹三最口腔肌肉训练记录为:5秒】

10. ***We ordered an egg salad sandwich, but the waitress brought us tuna fish*** 『金枪鱼』***instead.***

= We wanted a sandwich.

11. ***The doctor isn't in right now, but he should be back shortly*** 『不久;马上』.

= The doctor is not there.

{'elidʒibl}

12. ***His visa expires*** 『到期』***in November, but he is eligible*** 『有资格的;合格的』***to get a three-month extension*** 『延长;延期』.

= His visa expires in November.

13. ***Our family ordinarily goes camping on vacation, but this year we're***

going to take a tour 『观光旅行』.

= We usually go camping on our vacation.

14. *The food at the cafeteria* 『自助餐餐馆』 *is usually good, but last night it was awful* 『可怕的；极坏的；非常糟糕的』*.*

= The food at the cafeteria was bad last night.

15. *It isn't normally necessary to have an appointment in order to see the foreign student advisor, but during registration* 『登记注册』 *it's a good idea to make one.*

（和外国学生顾问见面一般是不需要事先预约的，但在登记注册这段时间，最好还是预约一下保险。）

= One should make an appointment with the foreign student advisor during registration.

16. *Cindy said that she could babysit any day but Friday.* = On Friday Cindy does not babysit.

【注】babysit：担任临时保姆；看守婴儿。

17. *I had just expected my daughter to come, but my son showed up too.*

（我只是等我女儿来，结果我的儿子也来了。）

= Both of my children came.

18. *Bill wanted to buy some cologne* 『科伦香水』 *for his wife's birthday, but the store didn't carry* 『（商店）具有；出售』 *the brand she usually uses.*

（比尔打算买科伦香水作为送给太太的生日礼物，但这家商店没有她经常使用的那个牌子。）

= Bill had planned to give his wife some cologne.

19. *Apartments near the University are very expensive,* *but we decided to rent one anyway, thinking that we would save money on gas* 『汽油』*.*

（大学附近的公寓非常昂贵，但我们还是决定租一套，想着我们会节省一些汽油钱。）

= Despite the expense 『经济上的负担；支出』, we rented an apartment near the University.

20. *There are fifty students scheduled for language lab* 『语言实验室』, *but there are only forty-five booths* 『摊位；小隔间』.

= Although there were only forty-five booths, fifty students wanted to take language lab.

21. *Although you are feeling better, I think that you should still see a doctor.*【生活中中肯、实用的建议】

= The speaker thinks that you should see a doctor.

22. *Although the weather is bad, the roads are clear.*

= The roads are clear 『畅通的』despite 『尽管；纵使』the bad weather.

23. *In spite of the problems, I doubt that Betty and Paul will get a divorce.*（尽管他们之间存在问题，但我怀疑贝蒂和保罗会离婚。）

= The speaker does not believe that Betty and Paul will get a divorce.

['resu(:)mei]

24. *From his resume* 『简历』, *this candidate appears to be well qualified for the job; even so, I think that we should check with his references* 『证明/介绍/推荐人（信）』.【高级精品句】

（从简历上看，这个候选人对于这项工作非常合格；即使是这样，我想我们还是应该核查一下他的推荐信。）

= The speaker thinks that he should check the candidate's letters of recommendation.

25. Students in the College of Architecture 『建筑学院』 **cannot graduate this semester unless they turn in** 『递交』 **their final projects** 『计划; 规划; 设计; 方案』 **by the end of the week.**

= Students who turn in their final projects by the end of the week will be able to graduate this semester.

26. Mr. Brown won't be able to work today, although Miss Smith will be there.

= Miss Smith will be there, but Mr. Brown won't.

27. Even though she insists that she was not offended, I am afraid she was.

= Despite her telling me that she was not offended 『冒犯; 触怒』, I believe that she was.

28. Although the rent includes water and gas, electricity costs about twenty dollars extra 『额外地』.

= You can expect to pay twenty dollars more than the rent 『租金』 for electricity.

29. Though Ellen can read quite well without her glasses, she needs them to see at a distance 『在稍远的地方』.

= Ellen uses her glasses to see far away.

30. The traffic was very light 『少量的; 轻微的』 **even though it was rush hour.**

= Despite its being rush hour 『交通拥挤时间』, there was little traffic.

31. Contrary to 『与⋯相反』 **what I had originally** 『原来;

最初』 *thought, the trip turned out* 『结果是；证明是』 *to be fun.*

（和我当初想像的正相反/出乎预料，这次旅行很有趣。）

= The trip was more fun than I thought it would be.

【高级精品句】

[sup]

32. Since there wasn't any tomato soup on the shelf, I bought beef stew instead.

= I bought stew 『炖菜』.

['indʒə]

33. In spite of his injury 『损伤；受伤』**, James was able to play football in the big game last Saturday.**

= James was able to play in the big game last Saturday even though he was injured.

34. Although my roommate is a very nice person, he's not my best friend. = My roommate is very nice, but he is not my best friend.

35. Ellen can't go to the University unless she gets a scholarship 『奖学金』**.**

= If Ellen gets a scholarship, she can attend the University.

36. Instead of going back to Florida, you ought to go to California this year.

= Although you usually go to Florida, this year you should go to California instead.

【李阳·克立兹三最口腔肌肉训练记录为：5 秒】

37. Anna already speaks English very well; even so, she wants to continue studying at the Institute 『学院』**.**

= Anna will continue studying at the Institute in spite of

speaking English well.

【李阳·克立兹三最口腔肌肉训练记录为:5秒】

38. Mr. Smith would not stop drinking even though the doctor told him that he must.

= Mr. Smith drinks in spite of his doctor's advice.

39. Although John never means 『意欲;打算』 to tell, he just can't keep a secret.

(约翰的嘴巴守不住/嘴松/嘴不紧。)

= John always tells 『泄露 (秘密);吐露 (真情)』 se-crets.

40. Since there aren't any tickets left for the concert, let's go to the movies instead of going back home.

(中国人说中国话的翻译最高境界:音乐会没票了,咱们去看电影吧,别回家了。)【高级精品句,脱口而出,倍感自豪！】

= We will go to the movies because we could not get tickets for the concert.

【李阳·克立兹三最口腔肌肉训练记录为:6秒】

Jaguar Sedan

第二节：小对话

第一部分：信息搜索

【短评】这个部分应该比较容易，答案就在对话中，只要能听懂，一般都可以选对。但问题是，在对话中出现多种信息，如果我们的听力比较薄弱，就可能会导致顾此失彼或是糊糊涂涂！关于这类题目有一些蒙混过关的技巧，但是克立兹还是主张：与其花费时间研究那些无聊的、也许有点用的技巧，不如刻苦练习英语真功夫！有什么技巧能比完全、轻松听懂更有效呢？

1. **W: John, I'm sorry to be so late. Thank you for waiting.**

   M: Oh, I didn't mind. I've only been here fifty minutes. You said that you might be as much as an hour late, so I just bought my newspaper and ordered myself a cup of coffee.

   （没关系，我才到了五十分钟。你说你可能会晚一个小时，所以我带上报纸并要了一杯咖啡。）

   Q: How long has the man been waiting?

   A: Fifty minutes.

   【李阳·克立兹三最口腔肌肉训练记录为：10秒】

2. **W: Are you glad that you came to Washington?**

M: Yes, indeed. I'd considered going to New York or Boston, but I've never regretted my decision.

（是的。我曾经考虑过去纽约或是波士顿，但我从来不后悔我的决定。）

Q: Where does the man live?

A: In Washington.

3. *M: Something is wrong with second gear*『（汽车的）排档』. *It seems to run fine in reverse*『倒车』, *and drive, but when I shift it into second, the motor stalls*『停止』*out.*

W: I hope that it won't be too difficult to fix.

Q: Which gear needs to be fixed?

A: Second gear.

【注】因为汽车在中国远远不普及，所以大多数人对汽车的常识很少，这样就导致这道听力题非常难！下面我们来学习一个有关汽车的重要词。

gear：齿轮组；汽车排档；传动装置

 * a car with five gears

 （一辆有五档的汽车）

 * She changed gears to make the car go up the hill faster.

 （她换了档，使汽车在上坡时快一点。）

 * A: The car isn't moving!

 B: That's because you're not in gear.

 （因为你没有上档。）

4. *W: You're always working around the house on Saturday, painting and doing repairs! You must enjoy it.*

（星期六你总是忙忙碌碌收拾房子，刷油漆，修修补补，你一定乐在其中。）

M: Not really. I'd rather relax or go fishing, but

Saturday is the only day I have to get anything done. By the time I get home from work during the week. I'm too tired.

(不见得。我宁愿放松放松或是去钓鱼，但星期六是唯一可以干点事的日子。平常工作完回到家里，已经太累了。)

Q: What does the man usually do on Saturdays?
A: He works at home.

【李阳·克立兹三最口腔肌肉训练记录为：11秒】

5. **W: The chocolate cake is very good today.**
   M: No thanks. I'll have apple pie with vanilla『香草』ice cream on top.
   Q: What kind of dessert did the man order?
   A: He ordered apple pie.

6. **M: The main library is open from eight A.M. until nine P.M. Monday through Friday; noon until six P.M. Saturday and Sunday; and twenty-four hours a day during finals『期末考试』week. This is a recording and will not repeat. If you need further assistance, please stay on the line until an operator answers.**

(大图书馆开放时间是：平日的早上八点至晚上九点；周六、周日的中午至下午六点；期末考试那一周全天二十四小时开放。这是录音，将不再重复，如需进一步的帮助，请不要挂电话，等待接线生与你联系。)

W: Hello. This is the operator. May I help you?
Q: When is the library open on weekdays『工作日』?
A: From eight o'clock in the morning until nine o'clock at night.

【李阳·克立兹三最口腔肌肉训练记录为：16秒】

7. M: Mr. Black is fluent in Spanish and now he's beginning to study Arabic.

　W: He also knows a few words in Japanese and Chinese.

　Q: Which language does Mr. Black speak well?

　A: Spanish.

8. M: I'm going to the museum Sunday afternoon. There's a new exhibit of Indian art from Arizona and New Mexico. Want to go with me?

　W: I'd love to, but my best friend is getting married on Sunday and I wouldn't miss it for anything 『无论如何也(不)』.

　　（我非常想去，但我最好的朋友星期天结婚，我是无论如何不会错过的。）

　Q: Where is the woman going on Sunday afternoon?

　A: To a wedding.

【李阳·克立兹三最口腔肌肉训练记录为：8秒】

9. M: These silver earrings『耳环』are only sixteen dollars this week. The gold ones are twenty-four.

　W: I'll take the silver ones, then; or, on second thought『再思之后』give me the gold ones. I have a gold necklace that would look very nice with them. [ˈneklɪs]

　Q: What did the woman decide to buy?

　A: She decided to buy a pair of gold earrings to match『相配；搭配』a gold necklace that she already had.

　　【注】＊ **On second thought(s)**, he decided to stay on the job.（重新考虑之后，他决定不辞掉他的工作。）

　　　＊ His necktie does not match his coat.

（他的领带和他的上衣不相配。）

10. **M:** *It only takes two hours to get to New York, but you'll have a six-hour layover*『中途停留』 *between flights.*

   W: *Oh, that's alright. I don't mind having the time in New York. I still have a few things to shop for.*

   Q: *How many hours will the woman be in New York?*

   A: *Six hours.*

11. **M:** *Are you sure that you brought your purse with you in the first place*『首先』*?*

   W: *Yes. I had it when I got in the car. I thought that I might have left it on the car seat, but when I went back it wasn't there. Maybe I put it down on the counter when I checked my coat outside the auditorium*『礼堂；会堂』*.*

   Q: *Where does the woman believe that she has left her purse?*

   A: *On the counter*『柜台』*.*

【李阳·克立兹三最口腔肌肉训练记录为：12 秒】

   【注】**check:**（领取号码牌）寄存…；托运（行李）

   ＊ Check your raincoat at the door.

   （把你的雨衣寄存在门口。）

12. **M:** *Do you have your Christmas shopping done yet?*
   （你完成圣诞节采购了吗？）

   W: *Almost. I got a watch for my husband, but I can't seem to find anything for my dad. He would probably like a book or a case*『箱子；盒子』 *for his coin collection*『硬币收集』*.*

   Q: *What did the woman buy her husband for*

Christmas?

A: She bought him a watch.

【李阳·克立兹三最口腔肌肉训练记录为：10秒】

13. *M: I feel obligated『使负义务』to attend the party, but really I'd much rather go with you to the concert.*

（我不得不去参加那个聚会，但我确实很想和你一起去听音乐会。）

W: I'm sorry that you can't. They will be playing music from the big band era『年代；时代』. ['iərə]

Q: Where is the woman going?

A: To a concert.

14. *M: Which dress do you plan to wear?*

W: I like the black one, and it fits me better, but it's probably too dressy『时髦的；考究的；讲究穿戴的』. I suppose I'll wear the red one.

Q: Why didn't the woman wear the black dress?

A: Because it is too formal for the occasion.

（对于那个场合太正式了。）

【李阳·克立兹三最口腔肌肉训练记录为：7秒】

15. *M: Have you started writing your paper for history?*

（你开始写历史课的研究报告了吗？）

W: Not yet. I'm still writing up my laboratory assignments『指定作业』for chemistry and studying for my midterms『期中考试』 in English and French.

Q: For which class must the woman begin to prepare?

A: She must begin writing a paper for her history class.

【李阳·克立兹三最口腔肌肉训练记录为：10秒】

67

第二部分:听力老一套——计算

【短评】就算是用中文对话,我们也需要时间反应和计算一下才能选择对答案,用英文就更难了。

下面一共为大家准备了十五段情景小对话,基本上概括了听力计算考题的主要"小把戏",现在的关键问题就是要:反复!反复!再反复!直至脱口而出并接近或达到,甚至超过李阳·克立兹的"三最"口腔肌肉训练记录。经过这样的千锤百炼,你再参加听力考试时,就一定会有全新的感觉!

Jeep Wrangler

1. **M: *Do you rent rooms by the week? You see, I'm not sure whether I'll stay for a whole month.***

   (你们按星期租房吗? 因为我不确信我是否会呆上整整一个月。)

   W: *Yes. The rates*『费用;价格』*are higher though. It's 50 dollars a week, but only 160 dollars a month.*

   Q: *How much will the man owe*『欠』*if he rents the room for three weeks?*

   A: *He will owe 150 dollars.*

   【李阳·克立兹三最口腔肌肉训练记录为:10秒】

   【注】通过上面这段对话,我们应该掌握一个重要词汇 **owe**。

   owe: 欠(债等);应该向(某人)付出;把…归功于;由于;感激;感恩。

   * I owe him ten dollars. (我欠他十美元。)

   * How much do you owe her?

（你欠她多少钱？）

* He owes his success to his hard work.

（他认为自己取得的成功是辛勤劳动的结果。）

* I owe you for your help.

（我感谢你的帮助。）

2. **W: Excuse me. I'm trying to get to the Student U-nion.**

M: Sure. Just go down here to the corner and turn left. Then go straight for three blocks and turn left at the tower. It's two blocks from there.

Q: How far must the woman walk to get to the Student Union?

A: She must walk five or six blocks『街区；一段街』.

【李阳·克立兹三最口腔肌肉训练记录为：11秒】

【注】这是典型的关于"**block**"的对话，**block**在听力考试中经常出现，在这里是指一个街区一边的距离，或是说两个街道之间的距离。它的另外一个意思是"由四条马路围成的方形楼房区"，或简称为"街区"。下面给大家三个典型例句，以便正确使用这个单词。

* The station is two blocks away.

（车站离这里有两个街区。）

* I live two blocks from the school.

（我住在离学校两个路口的地方。）

* We live in the same block.

（我们住在同一街区。）

69

3. **M: How much are the tickets?**

W: They're ten dollars each for the general public, but student tickets are half price.

（一般票价十美元，学生半价。）

Q: How much will the man pay for two general

tickets and two student tickets?

A: *The man will pay thirty dollars.*

【李阳·克立兹三最口腔肌肉训练记录为：7秒】

4. M: *How much are these sweaters*『毛线衣』?

 W: *They're on sale today, sir. Twenty-five dollars each, or two for forty dollars.*

 Q: *How much does one sweater cost?*

 A: *Twenty-five dollars.*

5. M: *I'd like to place a station-to-station call*『叫号的长途电话』 *to Ann Arbor please. How much will that be?*

 W: *That's fifty-five cents for the first three minutes, and ten cents for each additional*『附加的；追加的』*minute.*【王牌精品句】

 （前三分钟是五十五美分，以后是每分钟十美分。）

 Q: *How much will the man pay for a ten-minute call?*

 （打十分钟电话需要多少钱？）

 A: *He will pay ＄1.25.*【经典听力难题】

6. W: *Excuse me. Do you have the time?*

 （现在几点了？）

 M: *Yes ma'am. I have 1: 15, but my watch is a little bit fast.*

 Q: *What time is it?*

 A: *It is a little before 1: 15.*

 （不到一点一刻。）

 【李阳·克立兹三最口腔肌肉训练记录为：5秒】

7. W: *That's fifteen dollars, sir.*

 M: *I'd like to pay by check. May I make it out for more than that?*

 （我想用支票付帐，我可以多开吗？）

W: *Certainly. There's a ten-dollar limit over the amount of purchase, though.*

Q: *What is the maximum*『最大限度;最大量』*amount for which the man may write his check?*

A: *He may write a check for twenty-five dollars.*

【注】这个对话告诉我们一个国外的生活常识：limit 是商店为了避免顾客开支票付款时，超出购买总额过多，反增加找钱的麻烦，而作的限制。

ten-dollar limit 就是所开的支票，只能比购买的总金额多出十元。

另外，我们还需要掌握一个重要动词词组：**make out**。

make out: 书写;填写;开列。【中国人很难建立感情的短语】

* make out a check（开出支票）

* to make out a bill/a list（开列帐单/清单）

8. M: *Do I have enough postage*『邮资』*on this package?*

W: *Let's see. You already have three fifteen-cent stamps and two twenty-five cent stamps on it. You only need one five-cent stamp.*

Q: *What is the total amount of postage required to mail the package?*

A: *$ 1.00.*

【李阳·克立兹三最口腔肌肉训练记录为:9秒】

【注】邮局寄信或包裹计算邮费是一种听力常用的小把戏，这道题已经是非常难的了，因为里面包含了七个数字单词！请用"三最"法和"一口气"法疯狂操练，建立感情！

71

9. W: *I thought*『我原以为』*that these typewriter ribbons*『色带』*cost three dollars.*

M: *They used to, but the price has gone up fifty*

cents.

（它们以前是这个价,但现在价格升了五十美分。）

Q: **How much do the typewriter ribbons cost now?**

A: **They cost ＄3.50.**

【李阳·克立兹三最口腔肌肉训练记录为:6秒】

10. W: **Aren't there any direct flights?**

（有直达飞机/航班吗？）

M: **I'm sorry. Your best bet**『最佳的选择』**would be a nine A.M. departure on United flight twelve arriving in Chicago at eleven A.M., with a five-hour wait for your connecting**『相连的；衔接的』**flight to Los Angeles.**【听力特别难题】

Q: **What time will the woman leave Chicago?**

A: **At four o'clock.**

【李阳·克立兹三最口腔肌肉训练记录为:10秒】

【注】这是一道关于旅行转车/转机的典型题目。上面这道题属于比较难的一类,因为里面出现了"几点离开"、"航班号码"、"中转地点"、"到达时间"、"等待转机时间"、"最终目的地"等大量信息,如果没有英语真功夫,就会很容易产生混乱！

11. W: **I like these glasses, but they look like they would be quite expensive.**

（我喜欢这些,但它们看起来好像很贵。）

M: **They're 15 dollars a piece, or 150 dollars a dozen. Really that's not very expensive for genuine**『真正的』**leaded**『上含铅的釉的』**crystal**『水晶玻璃制品』.

Q: **How much does one glass cost?**

A: **15 dollars.**

【李阳·克立兹三最口腔肌肉训练记录为:8秒】

12. M: **My car gets forty miles per gallon.**

W: *Really? Mine only gets twenty.*

Q: *How does the man's mileage compare with that of the woman?*

A: *The man's mileage is twice that of the woman.*

【李阳·克立兹三最口腔肌肉训练记录为：7秒】

【注】这里有必要向大家解释一个 **mileage**。 *mile*=1.6 *km*

mileage：里数；里程；消耗一加仑汽油所行驶的里程。

13. M: *We don't have meters 『计量器』 here in Washington, because we have zones 『地区；同一收费区』. This is a two-zone ride, so the fare 『车费』 is $ 2.45.*

W: *Here's three dollars. Keep the change 『不用找钱』.*

Q: *How much did the woman give the driver as a tip 『小费』?*

A: *Fifty-five cents.*

14. M: *Miss Smith, I told Dr. Brown that I would call him in the Houston office at ten o'clock their time. Please find out the <u>time difference</u> for me so that I'll know when to place the call.*

（史密斯小姐，我告诉布朗博士，我将在当地时间十点致电其休斯顿办公室，请帮我查一下两地的时间差，以便我了解何时打电话给他。）

W: *It's two hours earlier in Houston, sir. I know without looking it up because my sister lives there.*

（休斯顿的时间比这里早两个小时。因为我妹妹住在那里，所以不用查我就知道。）

Q: *When should the man place his call to Houston?*

A: *At twelve o'clock.*

【李阳·克立兹三最口腔肌肉训练记录为：12秒】

73

【注】大家要特别注意并掌握"打电话"的不同说法，现在归纳如下：

1. make a phone call **2. telephone/phone**

3. call **4. call up** **5. place a call**

* My sister called me from Shanghai last night.

* I'll call you up later.

（我待会儿打电话给你。）

* I'll telephone/phone you this evening.

15. M: *Hello. This is Tom Davis. I have an appointment with Mrs. Jones for nine o'clock this morning, but I'm afraid I'll have to be about fifteen minutes late.*

W: *That's alright, Mr. Davis. She doesn't have another appointment scheduled until ten o'clock.* 【王牌精品句】

（没关系。琼斯夫人十点钟以前都有空／十点钟以前都没有其它的安排。）

Q: *When will Mr. Davis most probably meet with Mrs. Jones?*

A: *At 9: 15.*【从听力考试中获得实战能力】

【李阳·克立兹三最口腔肌肉训练记录为：11秒】

第三部分：听力老一套——猜地方

【短评】在这里需要再次强调一下，猜对地方真是很容易，根据对话中的"蛛丝马迹"，经常会在几乎没有听懂的情况下就猜出了对话发生的地点。但这又有什么用呢？实际生活和工作不是听力考试题，你花费大量的精力和金钱也不是为了只要猜对答案就万事大吉！我们需要英语真功夫！脱口而出、表达一切的真功夫！请用"三最"法猛烈轰炸下面的精彩对话，直至像母语一样脱口而出！你一定会让外国人刮目相看的：

你说英语和他们说母语一样地道流畅！我们只通过"大喊"听力考题就可以达到这样的辉煌！

Limo

1. **M:** *You'll be glad to know that no new cavities『洞；穴』have shown up on the X-rays『X 光照片』, Miss Smith.*

   W: *That is good news. I'll just have my teeth cleaned then.*

   （那真是好消息，那么就请给我洗牙。）

   Q: *Where did this conversation most probably take place?*

   A: *At a dentist's office.*

   【李阳·克立兹三最口腔肌肉训练记录为：7 秒】

   【注】在国外，由于生活习惯的影响，他们每天吃大量的甜食，于是牙齿问题成了一个日常主要担忧之一，牙医也就成为美国收入最高的职业之一。在听力考试中，"看牙齿"是一个常出现的情景。

2. **W:** *I'd like to get this prescription『药方；处方』refilled『再填满』please.*

   （我想按这个药方再配一次药。）

   M: *I'm sorry, Miss. This prescription can't be refilled. See, it says "no refill" right here on the label『标签』.*

   Q: *Where did this conversation most probably take place?*

   A: *In a drug store.*

   【注】prescription 是一个经常出现的重要单词，下面列出一些关于它的常用短语：

＊ make a prescription（开药方）

＊ have the prescription filled

= make up the prescription（抓药；配方）

＊ write out a prescription for（为…开药方）

＊ prescription drug（非经医生处方不得买卖的药品）

由此可见美国的医生权力非常大，所以会发生医生非法买卖处方的犯罪。

3. **W: Isn't Mary Ellen a beautiful bride?**

   M: She is indeed. John looks very happy too, doesn't he? He told me that they'll be going to Florida on their honeymoon.

   （真是漂亮！约翰显得非常快乐，不是吗？他告诉我他们要去佛罗里达州度蜜月。）

   Q: Where did this conversation most probably take place?

   A: At a wedding.

   【李阳·克立兹三最口腔肌肉训练记录为：7秒】

4. **W: Press twelve, please. Thank you.**

   M: You're welcome. That's where I'm going too.

   Q: Where did this conversation most probably take place?

   A: In an elevator.（在电梯里。）

5. **W: They'll call the doctoral candidates『博士候选人』names next. Have you found Larry yet?**

   M: No. They all look alike with those black robes 『礼服』on.

   Q: Where did this conversation most probably take place?

   A: At a graduation.

   【李阳·克立兹三最口腔肌肉训练记录为：6秒】

[ˈdounnt]

6. **W:** *I'd like a dozen glazed『光滑的』 doughnuts『油煎圈饼』and a loaf of French bread, please.*

   M: *Yes, ma'am. That's 3 dollars.*

   Q: *Where did this conversation most probably take place?*

   A: *In a bakery『面包店』.*

7. **W:** *What was that title again?*

   M: *"God is an Englishman." It's a very famous book. I'm sure you must have it.*

   Q: *Where did this conversation most probably take place?*

   A: *At a library.*

8. **W:** *Are these treatments really necessary? They don't seem to help very much.*

   （这些治疗必要吗？它们好像没有用。）

   M: *I'm afraid so, Mrs. Jones. Just be patient and I'm sure you'll see some results soon.*

   （恐怕是必要的，琼斯夫人。请耐心一点，我相信很快就会见效的。）

   Q: *Where did this conversation most probably take place?*

   A: *In a doctor's office.*

   【李阳·克立兹三最口腔肌肉训练记录为：8秒】

9. **W:** *We have several kinds of accounts『帐户』, Mr. Brown. The best interest rate is for the customer club account, but you must maintain a monthly balance『余额』of 300 dollars.*

   （我们这里有几种帐户，利息最高的是顾客俱乐部帐户，但是你必须保持三百美元的月余额。）

   M: *That will be fine.*

Q: *Where did this conversation most probably take place?*

A: *At a bank.*

10. W: *These tomatoes are huge! You must have watered them a lot!*

（这些番茄真大！你一定经常浇水。）

M: *Yes, I did. They ought to be <u>ripe</u> enough to pick by next Friday when we have our picnic.*

（是的。它们应该在下个星期五我们野餐时就可以摘了。）

Q: *Where did this conversation most probably take place?*

A: *In a garden.*

【李阳·克立兹三最口腔肌肉训练记录为：7秒】

11. M: *Could you please tell me what room Robert Davis is in?*

W: *Yes, he's in the <u>intensive care unit</u>『特别护理病房』on the fourth floor. I suggest that you <u>check with</u> the nurse's station『值班台』before going in, though.*

Q: *Where did this conversation most probably take place?*

A: *At a hospital.*

【李阳·克立兹三最口腔肌肉训练记录为：9秒】

12. W: *I just want a wash and <u>set</u>『卷头发』, please.*

M: *Fine. Why don't you let me blow dry『吹干』it this time instead of putting it up in rollers『卷轴；滚筒』? I think that you would like it that way.*

Q: *Where did this conversation most probably take place?*

A: *At a <u>beauty shop</u>『美容院』.*

13. **M:** *Good morning, Mary. How are you?*

   W: *Oh, fine. I'm just on my way to work, but I thought that I would drop by*『顺便办事、拜访』*with the check for my rent.*

   （我正要去上班，但我已打算顺便去您那里交付房租的支票。）

   Q: *Where did this conversation most probably take place?*

   A: *At an apartment building.*（在公寓大楼。）

   【注】check 是大家要努力去建立感情的词汇，因为在美国使用支票极其普遍，所以在听力考试中这个词经常出现，但由于没有生活经验做基础，一般人对此反应比较迟钝。下面给大家两个实用句子：

       * I always pay bills by check.

       （我总是用支票付帐）

       * My checkbook has two checks left.

       （我的支票簿还剩下两张。）

14. **W:** *The special*『特餐；特别介绍』*today is baked*『烤』*chicken and dressing*『调味品』*.*

   M: *No thank you. Just bring me a cup of coffee and the check*『帐单』*please.*

   Q: *Where did this conversation most probably take place?*

   A: *In a restaurant.*

15. **M:** *I've forgotten my passbook*『银行存折』*, but I'd like to make a deposit*『存款』*to my savings account*『储蓄帐户』*if I may.*

   （我没有带存折，但如果可能的话，我想存进去一笔钱。）

   W: *No problem. Just bring this receipt*『收据』 *with*

you the next time you come in, along with your passbook, and we will adjust『调整』the balance『差额』.

Q: *Where did this conversation most probably take place?*

A: *At a bank.*

【李阳·克立兹三最口腔肌肉训练记录为：9秒】

第四部分：听力大挑战——推理总结归纳提高

【短评】这类题目的答案不是非常明显，需要你在完全听懂的基础上进行一定的推理、总结、归纳和提高。通过对下面十五道经典试题的反复体会，你的听力能力会再次获得一个大的飞跃！

Mercedes 300SL

1. W: *How did your interview go?*

(你的面试情况怎样？)

M: *I couldn't feel better about it! The questions were very fair, and I seemed to find an answer for all of them.*

(我感觉再好不过了！问题非常公平，而且我似乎都能正确回答。)

Q: *What is the man's attitude『态度；看法』about the interview?*

A: *He is confident.*

【李阳·克立兹三最口腔肌肉训练记录为：6秒】

2. M: *I still haven't received my score『分数；成绩』on the GMAT test. Maybe I should call to check on*

it.

W: **Don't worry so much. It takes at least six weeks to receive your score.**

（别担心。至少需要六个星期才能收到分数。）

Q: **What does the woman think that the man should do?**

A: **She thinks that he should wait.**

【李阳·克立兹三最口腔肌肉训练记录为：8秒】

['vainil]

3. M: **These gloves are quite a bit cheaper than the leather ones. They are vinyl『乙烯树脂』, but frankly I can't tell much difference.**

（这些手套比皮革的便宜多了，它们是用乙烯树脂做的,但说实话,我也分辨不出来。）

W: **I really like the leather, but I can't pay twenty-six dollars.** ['leðə]

Q: **What will the woman probably do?**

A: **She will probably buy the vinyl gloves.**

4. W: **Do you think that Bob is serious about Sally?**

（你认为鲍伯对萨丽是认真的吗？）

M: **Well, I know this. I've never seen him go out so often with the same person.**

（我知道这件事的真相。我从来没有见过他如此频繁地和同样一个人约会。）

Q: **What conclusion does the man want us to draw from his statement?**

（这个男人想让我们从他的陈述中得出怎样的结论？）

A: **That Bob is serious about Sally.**

【李阳·克立兹三最口腔肌肉训练记录为：8秒】

5. W: **Whereas European nations have traditionally employed『采用；使用』metric『公制；米制』units** ['metrik]

81

such as meters and grams, the United States has employed English units such as feet and pounds.

（欧洲传统上采用了公制单位，比如说米和克，而美国采用了英式计量单位，比如说英尺和磅。）

M: Both systems are now in use in the U.S., though.

Q: What are these people most probably discussing?

A: Weights『重量』and measurements『量度』.

【李阳·克立兹三最口腔肌肉训练记录为：11秒】

　　【注】**whereas**: 然而；而；虽然

　　　　* He is short, whereas she is tall.

　　　　* Whereas he likes coffee, his wife does not like it very much.

　　　　（虽然他喜欢咖啡，他太太却不大喜欢。）

6. **W:** Jane told me that she was going to quit her job. I'll certainly be sorry to see her go.

　　M: Oh, she always says that! I wouldn't buy her a going-away present if I were you.

（她总是这么说！如果我是你，我才不会给她买送别礼物。）

　　Q: What does the man think about Jane?

　　A: That she will not quit her job.

7. **M:** I wonder what happened to Betty Thompson? I don't see her anywhere.

　　W: I don't know. She told me that she would be here at the play tonight.

　　Q: What do we learn『得知；获悉』about Betty from this conversation?

　　A: That she was not at the play.

8. M: I can't stand this class!

W: Well you might as well get used to it. It's required and you have to take『选修科目／课程』it in order to graduate.

(你最好慢慢习惯。这是必需的课程,如果你想毕业就不得不学习。)

Q: How does the man feel about the class?

A: He does not like it.

【注】may/might (just) as well:还是…的好;最好;倒不如。

9. M: I suppose we should look for a bigger house, but I don't see『知道；明白』how we can afford one right now.

(我想我们应该找一个大一点的房子,但我不知道我们怎么才能支付得起。)

W: If only we hadn't spent so much money on our vacation this year.

(要是我们今年度假没有花费那么多钱就好了。)

Q: Will the man and the woman buy a new house?

A: They will not buy a new house because they do not have enough money.

【李阳·克立兹三最口腔肌肉训练记录为:9秒】

10. W: Who's your new secretary, Tom?

M: Miss Evans. I'm very pleased with the work that she has done so far.

(到目前为止,我对她的工作非常满意。)

Q: What do we know about the man's secretary?

A: That the secretary has not been working there very long.

(秘书刚来不久。)

11. M: Your glasses are fine. If you don't like the

frames perhaps we could change them.

(你的眼镜不错。如果你不喜欢眼镜框的话,我们可以帮你换。)

W: Actually I was thinking of trying some <u>contact lenses,</u> *if you think that I would be able to wear them.*

(实际上我在考虑尝试一下戴隐形眼镜,如果你认为我适合的话。)

Q: To whom is the woman speaking?

A: To an <u>optometrist</u>『配镜师』. *optician* 眼镜商

12. *W: If I were you, I would take a plane instead of a bus. It will* <u>take you forever</u>『永远地』 *to get there.*

(如果我是你,我会坐飞机,乘巴士时间太久了。)

M: But flying makes me so nervous.

Q: What does the man prefer to do?

A: He prefers taking a bus because the plane makes him nervous.

【李阳·克立兹三最口腔肌肉训练记录为:7秒】

[ˈaiðə] [ˈiːðə]

13. *M: Weren't you in class Friday either?*

W: No. I had to take my mother to the airport. She went back to New York.

Q: What do we learn about the two students in this conversation?

A: That neither the man nor the woman was in class Friday.

(两个人星期五都没有去上课。)

14. *W: Maybe we should take Front Street this morning. The radio announcer said that traffic was very heavy*『交通拥挤』 *on the freeway*『高速公路』.

M: *Well, if he says to take Front Street we should go the other way!*

（如果他说走富朗特大街，我们就应该走另外一条路。）

Q: *What is the man's opinion of the radio announcer?*

A: *He does not believe what the announcer says.*

15. **M:** *If you don't have an account here, I can't cash your check. I'm sorry, but that's the way it is.*

（如果你在这里没有帐户，我不能兑现你的支票。很抱歉，事情就是这样。）

W: *Well, thanks a lot! You're a big help!*

（你真是帮了大忙！）【口语要素；"吓死"美国人】

Q: *How does the woman feel?*

A: *The woman is offended*『触怒；得罪』.

Rolls Royce

李阳·克立兹特别注解

碰到一个漂亮的单词，就赶紧将整个句子脱口而出，或是查字典，找出实用地道的例句，反复大喊，直至脱口而出。这样才能和这个单词建立深厚的感情，才算是真正掌握这个单词！

关于 **offend**，送给你几个句子：

1、Your words offended her.

（你说的话使她生气。）

2、I was very offended that you forgot my |

（你竟把我的生日也忘了，我很生气。）

从现在开始，你就成为 **offend** 这个单词的

85

第三节：混合集中轰炸一百例精选

【短评】前面进行了分类练习，使大家基本上了解了听力考试的各种小把戏，为攻克听力难关奠定了良好的基础。为了使大家的战斗能力更加强大、大脑反应更加迅速，现在我们进行混合集中轰炸练习。

第一部分:精彩一句话

1. ***Although the water was only four feet deep, it was over her head.***

   （虽然水只有四英尺深，但已经漫过了她的头。）

   = She must have been less than four feet tall.

   （她的身高一定不足四英尺。）

2. ***Stone does not want to go to work in his father's dental*『牙齿的；牙医的』*office.***

   （世通不想在他父亲的牙科诊所工作。）

   = Stone's father is a dentist.

3. ***The performance*『表演』*started at eight o'clock, and they were fifteen minutes late.***

= They got there at a quarter after eight.

4. _He was given a ticket because he drove past a stop sign._

= He got a ticket『交通违规通知单』for a traffic violation『违反行为』.

5. _She finally received her driver's license『驾驶执照』after her third try._

= She had tried unsuccessfully twice before.

6. _Actually, Frank's mother is my older sister._

= Frank is my nephew『外甥』.

7. _David cannot wait for his eighteenth birthday so he can get a driver's permit._

（大卫急不可待地盼望着十八岁的生日，以便拿到驾驶许可证。）

= One must be at least eighteen years old to get a driver's permit『许可（证）』.

8. _He paid 4,000 dollars for a new car; that's 500 dollars more than it would have cost last year._【王牌精品句】

（他花四千美元买了一辆新车，这个价格比去年的价格多了五百美元。）

= Last year's car would have cost 3,500 dollars.

9. _The avenues『大道；大街』of Manhattan are planned so that uptown『住宅区』is north and downtown『商业区；闹区』is south._

= An uptown train would be traveling north.

10. _She bought four pounds of tomatoes at seventy_

87

cents a pound.

= She paid $ 2.80 for the tomatoes.

11. **Like his father and his father's father, Alfred is an English teacher.**

= Alfred's grandfather was an English teacher.

12. **She enjoys shopping in the mall『购物中心』because there is more variety『变化；多样性』in the stores.**

= There are more different things in the stores in the mall.

13. **Some people travel great distances from home just to sit and watch the same television programs they always watch.**

（有些人旅行到很远的地方，但只是坐在那里看同样的、他们经常看的电视节目。）

= Some people watch their favorite programs wherever they are.

14. **His new boat is forty feet long, which is five feet longer than his old one.**

= His old boat was thirty-five feet long.

15. **To get to Denver you must change trains『倒车；换车』in Chicago.**

= The trains do not go directly to Denver.

16. **There has been a two-dollar increase in the bus fare; it now costs fourteen dollars one way.**

= The fare used to be twelve dollars.

17. **Emmy is a typical『典型的』 teenager; she loves to talk on the phone.**

= Most teenagers like to talk on the phone.

（大多数少年喜欢打电话聊天。）

18. The star quit『停止』the show two months before the end of her one-year contract『合同』.

= The star remained in the show for ten months.

19. The letter was returned unopened because the address on it was wrong.

（这封信被原封不动地退回，因为上面的地址写错了。）

= The letter had never been opened.

20. When everything else failed, he asked his father for more money.

（当没有其它任何出路时，他向他父亲要更多的钱。）

= He asked his father for more money after he had tried everything else.

21. Despite the advice of her physician『医师』, she continues to eat candy and cake.

= The lady consulted『请教；咨询』a doctor.

22. Because the liquor『酒类』stores were closed, they could not get champagne for the party. [ʃæmˈpeɪn]

['liːkə]

= They could not purchase the champagne because the stores were closed.

23. Marianne had lost her job; she could not afford to buy her son a present.

= Marianne could not afford to buy a present because she was out of work『失业』.

24. The Board of Directors『董事会；理事会』dismissed him because he had missed two consecutive『连续

89

的』 **meetings.**

= He was dismissed『开除；免职；解雇』 because he missed two meetings in a row『连续；接连』.

25. Laura lost five pounds on her diet『节食；减肥』, but her mother lost twice as much.

= Laura's mother lost ten pounds.

26. Some people feel that lighting three cigarettes on one match means bad luck.

（有人觉得／认为用一根火柴点燃三支香烟意味着恶运。）

= Some people feel that various things bring good or bad luck.

（有人觉得不同的东西会带来好的或坏的运气。）

27. Although this bag is much larger, that container『容器』 will hold more golf balls.

= Although the container is smaller, it will hold more golf balls.

28. She was able to go to work while her husband took care of the house.

（她丈夫料理家务以便她能够出去工作。）

= Her husband helped her by taking care of the house while she worked.

29. He refused to take his rubbers『橡胶套鞋』 with him even though it was raining.

= Although he knew it was raining, he did not wear his rubbers.

30. Stone felt that the reward『奖赏』 he was given really belonged to his friend.

（世通觉得他获得的奖励真正应该属于他的朋友。）

= Stone felt that he was unworthy of『不配的』the reward.

〔si：niə〕

31. **They displeased『使生气；使不快』the professor by quitting college in their senior year『大学四年级』.**

= The professor was displeased because they quit college『退学』.

32. **Herman put off『延期』writing his term paper『学期研究报告』until the last weekend.**

= Herman completed his term paper on the last weekend.

33. **She was lucky to find one garage『汽车修理厂』open during the holiday weekend.**

（她非常幸运,在周末找到营业的修理厂。）

= Almost all the garages were closed on the holiday weekend.

34. **It takes an hour to get home; you must leave now if you want to arrive by noon.**

（回家需要一个小时。如果你想中午之前到家,现在必须出发了。）

= It is now eleven o'clock.

35. **A baker's dozen『十三个』means one more than the exact number.**

= A baker's dozen actually amounts to『总计达』thirteen.

【注】baker's dozen 又作 long dozen,表示"十三个"。过去糕点师以及其他商店售货时以十三为一打,以免被控缺斤短两,所以产生这个说法。

91

36. **The manager crossed the item off the list.**

(经理将这个项目从目录中划掉。)

= He removed the item from the list by drawing a line across it.

【注】**cross ... off**：删去；剔除

* I crossed his name off the list.

(我从名单上删去他的名字。)

37. **She used to babysit while she was a freshman, but now she works at the library on campus.**

(在大学一年级时，她经常帮人看小孩，但是现在她在校园里的图书馆工作。)

= She has been working at the library rather than babysitting.

38. **On the bookshelf in the office is a dictionary for everyone's use.**

= Anybody can use the dictionary in the office.

39. **It would be a good idea to look into the company before you invest all your money.**

= Investigating the company before investing your money is a must『必须听、看、做的事』.

40. **I want to contact a friend of mine immediately, but I have no way of knowing where she lives.**

= I don't know and am not able to find out where she lives.

(我不知道也无法找到她住在哪里。)

41. **I prefer to work with a manager who speaks straight from the shoulder『从正面；直接地；不客气地』.**

(我比较喜欢和一位讲话坦率的经理工作。)

= The manager speaks frankly.

42. Although she already had a lot of work to do, she took on『承担』more responsibilities.

（虽然她已经有一大堆工作要做，她还是承担了更多的责任。）

= She undertook more responsibilities.

43. The forecast is for morning showers『阵雨』, light westerly『从西边吹来的』winds and possibly some snow by noon.【经典听力考题】

= It's expected to be rainy『下雨的；多雨的』, a little windy and cold.

44. Last year I commuted『定期往返；走读』to school from my home but this year I am living in a school dormitory.

= I traveled regularly between home and school last year.

45. We are looking forward to the vacation which will last a couple of weeks.

= We have a few weeks vacation.

46. He dropped Nancy off at her house.【简单但不容易听懂的句子】

= He took Nancy home.

47. She's been chosen to represent our class on the committee.

（她被选为委员会里我们班级的代表／她将代表我们班级加入委员会。）

= She will represent us on the committee.

48. **It feels warm today, but spring is still a month away.**

= In a month, we will have spring.

49. **Bill is going to present his paper at the Third International Graphic Symposium this morning.**

（比尔将在今天早上举行的第三届国际绘画研讨会上发表他的论文。）

= Bill's presentation is today.

50. **Nancy would like to increase her typing speed to get a better job, and so would I.**

= We both would like to type faster.

第二部分:情景小对话

1. **M: I hope you don't mind, but I want very much to watch the game this coming Sunday.**

   W: I certainly do mind, but there's not very much I can do about it, it there?

   （我当然介意,但又有什么办法/又能怎样?）

   Q: What was the woman objecting to?

   A: Her husband's watching a game.

   【注】**object to:** 反对;唱反调。

   * I object to the plan.

   * My parents objected to my climbing the mountain alone.

   （我父母反对我单独爬那座山。）

2. **W:** *What a strange suit*『一套衣服；套装』*you are wearing. Your jacket doesn't match your pants.*

   M: *I know. I got dressed in the dark, and I didn't realize my mistake until I had gotten to the office.*

   （我在黑暗中穿的衣服，一直到办公室我才发现这个错误。）

   Q: *Why does the man's suit seem unusual*『不寻常的；奇异的』*?*

   A: *The jacket and pants do not match*『搭配』*.*

3. **W:** *I was going to run in the Park Marathon. Then I read the forecast*『预报』*of heavy snow, and I decided not to go.*

   M: *It's a good thing you didn't. I ran there, and I almost froze to death.*

   （幸亏你没去,我到那里跑步,差点儿没被冻死。）

   Q: *What had the woman decided not to do?*

   A: *To run.*

4. **M:** *Hello. Will you please send someone up to my apartment. The hot water is running, and I can't turn it off.*

   （请派人上我的公寓来,这里的热水无法关闭。）

   W: *There's no one in the office right now. I'll send someone up as soon as I can.*

   Q: *Why did the man want someone to come up*『前来』*to his apartment?*

   A: *The water was running.*

5. **M:** *Can you give me some information about the cost of a trip to Los Angeles?*

   W: *I'm sorry, sir. I can't give you that information over the phone. The travel agent*『旅行社职员』

95

will be able to help you.

Q: *Where did the man want to go?*

A: *To Los Angeles.*

6. W: *I just bought this fake-fur*『仿毛皮』*coat at a sale* 『廉售；贱卖』*. I paid only 240 dollars for it. How do you like it?*

   M: *It's very nice, but my wife bought the same thing for half the price.*

   Q: *How much did the man's wife pay for her coat?*

   A: *120 dollars.*

7. W: *I really can't stand the way Harry dominates*『支 配；控制；统治』*the conversation all the time. If he's going to be at the party, I just won't come.*

   （我实在无法忍受哈利的个人中心主义，如果他要 参加这个晚会，我就不去了。）

   M: *I'm sorry you feel that way, but my wife insists that he come.*

   （很抱歉你这样想，但我妻子坚持要他参加。）

   Q: *Why is Harry being invited to the party?*

   A: *To please the man's wife.*

8. M: *I can come to your house and pick you up in half an hour. Is that all right?*

   （我半个小时以后去你家里接你，好吗？）

   W: *Good. That means you'll be here at eight-thirty.*

   Q: *What time is it now?*

   A: *Eight o'clock.*

9. M: *This is a very expensive watch, but I've had trouble with it ever since I bought it. I insist on* 『坚持；强调』*seeing the manager.*

   （这是一块昂贵的表，自从我买的那一天起就经常出问题。我一定要见经理。）

W: Actually, there is no need for that, sir. I'll give you another watch just like this one.

Q: Where did the conversation probably take place?

A: In a store.

10. W: My son finds it very difficult to be away from home. I'm afraid that he will drop out of college.

（我儿子离开家以后生存能力非常差，我担心他会中途退学。）

M: I had a similar problem with my older son. But he managed to adjust『调整；使适应』and stayed in school until he graduated.

（我的大儿子也有过同样的问题，但他成功地调整了自己，并顺利地毕业。）

Q: Where is the woman's son at the present time?

A: At a distant college.

11. M: I read the review『评论』 of this play. I must say that I disagree completely with the critic's dislike of the work.

（我读了这出戏剧的评论，我必须说，我完全不同意评论家对它的批评。）

W: Oh, that's funny. I read that review also, and I agree completely with his opinion.

Q: What was the woman's reaction to the play?

A: She dislike it.【听力典型难题】

12. W: My mother will be coming to visit us over the weekend, dear. It's been quite some time since she last saw her granddaughter.

（我母亲周末要来看我们，她已经很久没有和孙女见面了。）【注意翻译技巧】

M: Well, it will be a little crowded, but I've really

missed seeing your mother. That will be just fine.

Q: *Who is coming to visit the family?*

A: *The man's mother-in-law『岳母』.*

13. **W:** *I'm afraid I paid too much for these presents, but I just can't stand the thought of driving all the way back to the store to return them.*

（恐怕这些礼物我买贵了，但一想到要开车那么远去商店退货，真是让人受不了/恐惧。）

M: *Well, I'll be glad to take care of that a little later on.*

（过一小会儿，我将非常高兴/乐意帮你处理此事。）

Q: *How will the man get to the store to return the gifts?*

A: *He will drive.*

【注】later on: 以后；其后；稍后；待会儿

　　　＊ Let's discuss the plan later on.【口语要素】

14. **M:** *Our rent is now just 600 dollars a month.*

W: *I know. It's exactly one-third more than it was when we first moved in.*（我知道。这比我们刚刚搬进来时整整贵了三分之一。）

Q: *How much rent had been paid at first?*

A: *450 dollars.*

【注】这是最难的一种计算题！如果是数学很好的人，也许可以马上心算出来，但对于一般人，我还是建议你用简单的方程式来计算，这样保险。假设刚搬进来时的房租为 X 元，那么 $X + 1/3X = 600, X = 450$ 元。

15. **W:** *I certainly hope that this film is worthwhile. My feet are freezing『冻僵』, and I can't stand the cold much longer.*

M: *I hate standing in line anyway. If we don't get in soon, let's just forget it and go somewhere else.*

（我讨厌排队！如果我们过一会儿还进不去，那就算了，让我们到别处去吧。）

Q: *Where are the man and woman at this moment?*

A: *In line outside a movie house.*

16. W: *Even though he doesn't particularly like it, I insist on shoveling*『用铲子挖』 *the walk*『人行道』 *instead of letting my husband do it.*

M: *Well, that's the smart thing to do. After all, he had a heart attack not too long ago.*

（那样做很明智，毕竟，他不久前才心脏病突然发作。）

Q: *What is the husband's feeling about his wife doing the shoveling?*

A: *He does not like her doing it.*

17. M: *For the fourth time in a row*『连续』 *the German team has won the bobsled*『长橇；雪橇』 *race at the Winter Olympics.*

W: *Good for them. But I really can't get excited about that sport.*

（真不错！但我确实对那项运动不感兴趣／没有热情。）

Q: *How many times before had the German team won the bobsled race?*

A: *Three times.*

【注】在这里我们必须掌握一个重要的口语要素"**Good for you**/him/them..."，它表示"干得好"、"真棒"、"说得对"等意思。

18. W: *I understand you've become a real cook lately,*

Frank.

M: *Well, since my wife began working, I decided to help out*『协助』*by making the meals every once in a while*『偶尔』*.*

Q: *How frequently does Frank do the cooking at home?*

A: *Occasionally.*

19. W: *My son feels very discouraged because he did not make*『成为一员；获得职位』*the swimming team this year.*

M: *I can understand that. It took me at least three tries*『尝试；努力』*before I got on my college team.*

（我完全可以理解。我努力了三次才加入我们的大学队。）

Q: *What was the cause of the son's discouragement?*

A: *Failing to make the team.*

20. M: *I was so angered*『触怒；激怒』*when the cab driver tried to overcharge*『索价过高』*me that I called a policeman.*

（当那个出租汽车司机企图"宰"我的时候，我非常气愤，于是叫来了警察。）

W: *That kind of thing seems to be happening quite frequently. I think you did the right thing.*

（这类事情好像经常发生。你做得对！）

Q: *Why was the man annoyed*『生气；烦恼』*?*

A: *Because the driver charged too much.*

21. M: *If you had waited until after the Christmas holidays, you could have bought that dress for much less.*

（如果你等到圣诞节以后去买，这件衣服可以便宜得多。）【高难度精品句】

W: I know that, but I needed it immediately. I had a wedding reception『结婚喜宴』to attend.

Q: When had the woman purchased the dress?

A: During the Christmas season.

22. W: Is this the complaint department『顾客意见接纳部』? I'd like to speak to a supervisor『监督者；管理人』.

M: If you will hold the phone, Madam, I'll get Mr. Stone.

Q: What is Mr. Stone's position?

A: He is a suppervisor.

23. M: Why did you buy that atrocious『讨厌的；恶劣的』-looking hat? You know that green is not a good color for you.

W: Well, I thought this particular shade『色调；颜色深浅』wouldn't be too bad.

Q: What was the color of the hat the woman bought?

A: Green.

24. W: I have eaten in so many restaurants during the past week that the thought of eating out again makes me weak.

（在过去一个星期中，我吃了那么多饭馆，所以一想到又要出去吃饭，我简直两腿发软。）

M: I feel the same way, but there is no way to get out of this appointment.

（我有同感，但问题是现在没办法取消这个应酬／约会。）

Q: How do the man's feelings compare with those

101

of the woman?

A: *He agrees with her.*

25. M: *The family who controls the business feels that the firm will lose its independence if that huge conglomerate*『综合企业；集团企业』*takes it over*『接收；接管』.

〖kən'glɑmərɪt〗 紧张的同意书词

（控制这家企业的家族觉得，如果被联合大企业接收，这家公司将失去独立。）

W: *I understand*『听说；闻知』*that many of the stockholders are upset by the action, too.*

（据我所知，很多股东都对此收购行动表示忧虑。）

Q: *What is the cause of concern to the family in control?*

A: *That the firm will lose its independence.*

26. W: *Do you think that the possibility of cold weather and snow will affect the results of the game?*

（你认为可能的寒冷天气和下雪会影响比赛的结果吗？）

M: *Well, they are accustomed to playing in bad weather, so it shouldn't make any difference to them.*

（他们习惯于在恶劣的天气条件下比赛，所以应该不会造成影响。）

Q: *How do the man's feelings compare with those of the woman?*

A: *He thinks the weather will not make any difference.*

【注】一定要彻底掌握"**affect**"这个王牌动词！

＊ The hot weather affected his health.

（炎热的天气影响了他的健康。）

＊ He was deeply affected by what he heard.

（他听到那些话深受感动。）

three-fourth

27. **W: Three out of four critics blamed the director for the failure of that musical『音乐电影』.**

    M: That's one of the problems of being a director. You get blamed for every fault.

    （那就是做导演的麻烦之一，无论出什么问题，你都会受到责难。）

    Q: What had happened to the musical being discussed?

    A: It was a flop『大失败』.【重要单词】

28. **W: Do you want me to explain those problems before your exam?**

    M: What's the point『重要性；意义』? I don't understand a thing.

    Q: What does the man mean?

    A: He can't learn the material『资料』.

29. **W: I can't stand this apartment because the rent went up very high. So I am going to move out next week. Do you think you can give me a hand?**

    M: Don't worry. I'll ask my club members to see if some of them are free also.

    （没问题。我会问问我的俱乐部会员，看他们有没有人也有空。）

    Q: What does the man suggest?

    A: Trying to find others to help her too.

30. **M: The fabulous『非常了不起的；惊人的』 opera singers from Austria took New York by storm『强烈感染；大为轰动；使神魂颠倒』.**

    （从奥地利来的惊人的歌剧演唱家风靡了纽约。）

    W: Really, I would love to fly to New York and see

them now.

Q: *What does the man mean?*

A: *The opera singers were very popular with New Yorkers.*

31. M: *If you want to talk about a topic for your term paper, why don't you come back at 3 this afternoon.*

（假如你想讨论你学期报告的主题，何不下午三点回来？）

W: *Thank you. I hope my request isn't inconvenient for you.*

（谢谢你。希望我的要求不会令你有所不便。）

Q: *What does the woman mean?*

A: *She doesn't want to trouble him.*

32. M: *Which book will sell the most copies?*

（哪本书会卖得最多？）

W: *I am afraid I have no idea which book will sell.*

（我恐怕不知道哪一本书会有销路。）

Q: *What is the man asking about?*

A: *The title of the book published the most.*

33. W: *Where's that Italian restaurant that used to be here?*

（以前在这里的那家意大利餐厅哪里去了？）

M: *It burned to the ground last December.*

（它去年十二月烧为灰烬了。）

Q: *What does the man mean?*

A: *The restaurant was entirely destroyed by fire.*

34. M: *Now what's become of*『发生；变成；结局是』*my fork?*

（我的叉子在哪里啊？）

W: *There it is under your napkin*『餐巾』.

Q: *What is the man doing?*

A: *He is looking for his fork.*

35. M: *Could you tell me what the qualifications are for applying for financial assistance?*

(你能告诉我申请补助要什么资格吗？)

W: *Yes. Anyone who has a B average can apply for a scholarship if he needs financial aid.*

(只要是平均成绩为 B 等的人，如果需要财务援助，都可以申请奖学金。)

Q: *What does the woman mean?*

A: *To apply for a scholarship, one needs a B average.*

36. W: *We can't live without comput- ers these days, can we?*

(现在我们没有电脑就没法生存了,是不是？)

M: *Yes, but the important thing to remember is that we've got to become its master.*

(是的,但要切记的是,我们必须当电脑的主人。)

Q: *What does the man mean?*

A: *We cannot let computers control us.*

37. W: *I wonder why the electricity went out*『停电』*this morning.*

M: *It happened because of an oversight*『疏忽』*on the part of the engineer.*

(停电是因为工程师的疏忽。)

Q: *Why did the electricity go out?*

A: *Because the engineer made an error.* {erə}

38. M: *I'm sorry I was thinking about something else. What did you say?*

W: Oh, I was just thinking aloud.

（哦，刚刚我只是自言自语而已。）

Q: What does the woman mean?

A: She was talking to herself.

39. *W: I ran out of both salt and pepper.*

（我的盐和胡椒都用完了。）

M: I'll pick them up on my way home from work.

（下班回家的路上我会顺便买。）

Q: What will the man do?

A: Stop at the grocery store.

40. *W: Are you coming to Susan's birthday party at my house?*

M: I'll see because I've just gotten over the flu.

（再看看，因为我感冒刚好。）

Q: What does the man mean?

A: He is no longer ill but he wants to take care of himself.

41. *W: Guess what! I saw the rock singer in a downtown restaurant today.*

（猜猜看我遇见谁了！今天在市区的一家餐厅我看见那个摇滚歌星。）

M: You thought it was him but he is supposed to be in San Francisco for his concert tour.

（你认为看到的就是他，不过他应该是在旧金山做巡回演唱。）

Q: What does the man imply?

A: The woman may have made a mistake.

42. *W: I heard Mary has been invited to another dinner party, but I'm sure I invited her first.*

（我听说玛丽受邀参加另一个晚宴，但我确定是我先邀请她的。)

M: *Well, she is more likely to attend your party than the other one.*

(放心啦，她比较可能参加你的宴会，而不是那一个。)

Q: *What does the man mean?*

A: *Mary will probably come to the woman's party.*

43. **M:** *Do you have room for this small one?*

(你有地方放这个小东西吗？)

W: *Let me see. Oh maybe I could squeeze it in my cosmetic case.*

(让我看看。喔，或许我可以把它塞进我的化妆箱里。)

Q: *What is the man asking the woman?*

A: *To put one small item in her suitcase.*

44. **M:** *Did you hear that Bob got sick yesterday during the final examination?*

(你听说鲍勃昨天期末考试时生病了没有？)

W: *Yes, I did. I think lately he has bitten off more than he can chew in studying and working.*

(我认为他最近在学习和工作方面，都自不量力/过分辛苦了。)

Q: *What does the woman mean?*

A: *Bob is trying to study and work too much.*

45. **W:** *What's the matter with you today?*

M: *Oh boy. I've got a terrible hangover 『宿醉』.*

(喔，天啊。我酒喝得太多，头痛死了。)

Q: *What's the man's problem?*

A: *He doesn't feel well because he drank too much.*

46. **W:** *Why are you so provoked?*

（为何你如此愤怒？）

M: I had to study for tomorrow's biology test but Robert had the nerve to listen to the stereo for two hours.

（我必须准备明天的生物考试，而罗勃特竟厚颜地足足听了两小时的音乐。）

Q: What does the man mean about Robert?

A: He is impudent『厚颜的；鲁莽的；目中无人的』.

【注】为了和 "**have the nerve to do**" 建立更深厚的感情,请脱口而出下面这个句子:

△ * He had the nerve to ask me a very personal question.

（他竟厚起脸皮来问我一个隐私问题。）

47. **W:** Was I supposed to type this report this week?

（我应该这礼拜打这份报告吗？）

M: No, I assigned it to Mary. Why don't you type these proposals for the meeting next weeks?

（不用,我把它交给玛丽了。你可以打下星期开会时要用的议案。）

Q: What is Mary going to do this week?

A: She will type the report.

48. **W:** I think this dress is too expensive.

M: You can have it for 12 dollars with a pair of socks thrown in.

（可以卖你十二元,附赠一双短袜。）

Q: What does the man mean?

A: She can have free socks if she pays him 12 dollars for the dress.

【注】**throw in**:额外赠送。

▷ * They threw in this pen when I bought a bag.

（我买袋子时,他们附送了这支笔。）

49. M: *I thought it was Peter who was with yo*
day.

(我原以为昨天跟你在一起的是彼得。)

W: *That couldn't have been Peter because I*
seen him for ages.【包含难语法的高级精品

(那不可能是彼得,因为我已经好久没看到他

Q: *What does the woman mean?*

A: *The man must have been mistaken.*

50. W: *Have you decided to take that position in Chin*
Since they require Chinese, you won't have an
problem because you took it in high school,
didn't you? ↘

(你决定接受在中国的那份工作了吗? 既然他们需
要会说中文的人,你应该不会有问题,因为你高中
时已修过中文,不是吗?)

M: *I'd be all right if they only required a reading or*
writing knowledge of it. I could brush up in no
time, but you see, I have to speak there.

(假如他们只需要读或写中文,我没问题。我可以立
刻温习,但是你知道,我在那里必须说中文。)

Q: *What did the man say about reading and writing*
Chinese?

A: *He can review them in a short period of time.*

第四节：实战演习四套(托福标准)

在这一节里，我们为大家提供了四套托福听力全真试题原文，不需要大家去选择，只要求大家按照"句子疯狂处理三步骤"进行反复刻苦操练，直至和这些句子建立起像母语一样深厚的感情！

学一句算一句,时刻都有成就感！

第　一　套

Part A

1. Carol expected to go and so did Frank.

= Frank wanted to go.

2. Larry came home at 9: 00, but Dick and Tom didn't arrive until 10: 30.

= Dick came home at 10:30.

【注】再次请大家和"**not...until**"建立感情。上面的这个句子可以翻译成"一直到十点半才回来"。以后要尽量使用这个地道的句型。

* He did not come home／ back until late in the evening.

3. The singer was surprised that they liked his old songs but not his new ones.

= They liked his old songs.

4. While Bob played the piano his sister did his homework for him.

= His sister did Bob's homework.

5. They should have called by now if they aren't coming.

= They haven't called.

【注】对于难点单词和语法,李阳·克立兹系列英语突破书籍会反复讲解,反复刺激你的大脑,直至彻底掌握,立刻反应! 这里再次请大家注意一个重要的英语用法:**should have done**! 这个句子指的是过去的事情,如果是肯定句,说明某件事本应完成而未完成;如果是否定句,表示发生了不应当发生的事情。如:

* You should have stopped at the red light.

(看见红灯你就应该停车。)

* You should not have gone back to work without the doctor's permission.

(你不应该未经医生许可就回去工作。)

6. Sue's red and blue sweater is as nice as Mary's black one or Betty's orange one.

= Mary has a black sweater.

7. The books are 15 dollars, the pen 1 dollar, and the notebooks 2 dollars.

= The total is 18 dollars.

8. John drove to Chicago and then Ed drove to Detroit.

= John drove to Chicago.

9. *John sent a package『包裹』to his father and a letter to his mother.*

= He sent a package to his father.

10. *Unless Robert goes to school he won't see Ted or Jack today.*

（除非罗伯特去学校，否则他今天见不到泰德或是杰克。）

= Ted is at school.

11. *Charles is a better student than Paul but not than Ed.*

= Ed is the best student.【经典听力难题】

12. *Pam's cat was taken by Chuck or Gail.*

= Somebody took Pam's cat.

13. *If you see Richard, tell him the teacher wants him.*

= The teacher wants to see Richard.

14. *When my sister first got here Bob was still here.*

（当我妹妹刚到这里的时候，鲍伯还在这里。）

= My sister is here.

15. *Mary had to wait for Mike to call Rose and Henry.*

= Mike called Rose.

16. *Sue was told John got hit by Bill.*

= Bill hit John.

17. *The movie starts at 8：00, but Phil works until 8：30 and Jack until 9：30.*【测试你对数字的敏感】

= The movie starts at 8：00.

18. *Jim wanted to go, but his father said he shouldn't.*

    = Jim wants to go.

19. *There's a book on the table, another on the chair, and two on the floor.*

    = There are four books all together.

20. *If my brother gets ten more dollars, he'll have fifty.*

    = He has 40 dollars.

Part B

21. **W:** *Be careful. That car is coming very fast.*

    M: *You have to keep an eye out for*『密切注意』*motorcycles, too.*

    Q: *What does the man mean?*

    A: *That motorcycles can be dangerous.*

22. **M:** *The pants*『（美口）裤子』*are 10 dollars and the shirt is 6 dollars.*

    W: *Here's a twenty-dollar bill.*

    Q: *How much change will the woman get?*

    A: *4 dollars.*

23. **W:** *Hello, Mr. Jones. This is Betty Smith. May I speak to my husband?*

    M: *John is in the lab now, Betty. And then he's going to eat lunch. I'll tell him to call you at home.*

    Q: *Where is the woman's husband?*

    A: *In the lab*『（口）实验室；研究室』*.*

24. **M:** *I really like this black necktie.*

    W: *But the blue or gold one will look much nicer*

113

with your brown suit.

Q: What color necktie does the man want?

A: Black.

25. W: I wonder if John will be here by 8: 00. He's supposed to『应该』be.

M: His wife said he left at 7: 30, so he should be here by 8: 15 at the latest『最迟』.

Q: What time is John supposed to arrive?

A: 8: 00.

【李阳·克立兹三最口腔肌肉训练记录为:7秒】

26. M: Henry has four classes on Wednesday and Peter has three.

W: I only have two, but I have five on Thursday.

Q: How many classes does Peter have on Wednesday?

A: Three.

27. W: Are you going to the Johnson's party tomorrow night?

M: I don't think so. I have to work and my wife will be out of town.

Q: Why isn't the man going to the party?

A: He has to work.

【李阳·克立兹三最口腔肌肉训练记录为:5秒】

28. M: I was wearing my glasses a little while ago, but now I can't find them.

W: They must be upstairs because they aren't on the table or cabinet.

Q: Where are the man's glasses?

A: Upstairs.

29. **W:** *Have you seen Mr. Brown? He usually is here by 9: 00.*

   M: *He said he was coming at 9: 30 today, but it's already 10: 00. I wonder where he is.*

   Q: *What time does Mr. Brown usually come?*

   A: *9: 00.*

30. **M:** *Can you tell me where to find aspirin?* [ail]

   W: *That will be in the third <u>aisle</u>*『（超级市场等的）通道；过道；走廊』*to your left.*

   Q: *Where did this conversation probably take place?*

   A: *In a drugstore*『杂货店；药店』.

31. **W:** *Have you seen my brother? I can't find him any place.*

   M: *I saw him leaving with Phil and Don just a few minutes ago.*

   Q: *Who is the woman looking for?*

   A: *Her brother.*

32. **M:** *Do you think Ed will get here on time?*

   W: *If Ed doesn't, nobody will.*

   【最简单的句子表达最丰富、强烈的含义】

   （如果爱德不准时来，没人能够准时。）

   Q: *What does the woman mean?*

   A: *She thinks Ed will be on time.*

33. **W:** *Have you heard if Frank is coming back today?*

   M: *He was supposed to arrive next week, but he's coming <u>the day after tomorrow</u>.*

   （他原本应该下周回来的，但现在他将会后天到达。）

   Q: *When will Frank arrive?*

115

A: *The day after tomorrow.*

34. M: *I don't like Mozart as well as Bach or Beethoven.* [bak] {bi:tovən}

    W: *Oh, I do. And I like Strauss even better.*

    Q: *Who does the woman like the best?*

    A: *Strauss.*

35. W: *Aren't you going to work today?*

    M: *I called my boss and said I was sick. I'm going to play golf with Bill.*

    Q: *Why isn't the man going to work?*

    A: *He's going to play golf.*

Part C

Questions 36 to 39 are based on the following conversation between a customer and a clerk in a department store『百货商店』.

A: *Could you help me please? I'm looking for something for my husband's birthday next week and I just can't seem to think of anything to buy.*

B: *Certainly, Ma'am. You don't have anything special in mind?*

（你没有什么特别的打算/计划/想法吗？）

A: *Right. I just don't know ...*   Italian [itæljən]

B: *How about a nice silk tie? We have some handsome 『漂亮的；美观的』 ties that just arrived from Italy.* [itli]

A: *Not a tie. I gave him one for Christmas and he has never worn it. He hates ties. He would never speak to me again if I gave him another one.*

B: *I see. Perhaps, then, a set of cuff links『（衬衫的）袖扣』and a nice tie tack『（美）领带针』.*

A: *I just said he doesn't wear ties.*

B: *Of course. This is a very nice matched『相配的』set*

of men's cosmetics 『化妆品』*- after-shave, cologne* 『科伦香水』*, and talcum powder*『（化妆 用的）粉；爽身粉』.

A: *I don't know. My husband has never used that kind of thing very often. He might not care for*『喜欢』*that either. Can you think of anything else?*

B: *I believe I have just the thing. This billfold*『钱包/夹』*is something any man would be proud to own. It has this section of plastic windows for pictures and things. There are also several pockets for credit cards and a very deep money pocket. It's made of the very finest leather.*

A: *That does sound nice. Please gift wrap*『以礼品形式包装』*it. And would you put this card in with it?*

B: *Certainly, ma'am. It will take just a few minutes.*

A: *All right. I'll wait.*

【李阳・克立兹三最口腔肌肉训练记录为：60秒】
【李阳・克立兹一口气底气训练记录为：4 口气】

36. Q: Why does the woman want to buy something for her husband?

    A: It's a birthday present.

37. Q: What kind of present did the woman give her husband the last time?

    A: A tie.

38. Q: What does the woman say about men's cosmetics?

    A: Her husband doesn't use them often.

39. Q: Why does the clerk recommend the billfold?

    A: It has a very deep money pocket.

Questions 40 to 43 are based on the following conversation between a man and a woman at an office.

A: *Jean, were you able to get that report all* <u>*typed up*</u>*.*
（那份报告打完了吗？）

B: *Not yet, Mr. Black. Mrs. Grant asked me to type some letters for her. I'll be finished pretty quick and then I'll start on that.*

A: *Don't forget I need it first thing*『（口语）首先；第一件事是』*in the morning. I have to take it along to Chicago to the regional meeting.*

B: *Don't worry, I'll get it done. My husband's on a business trip*『出差』*too. He's in Detroit today, and tomorrow he'll be in Boston. So I'm planning to stay late. After it's typed up I'll leave it on your desk. I should be finished by 8: 00.*

A: *I'm sorry to keep you so late.*【高级口语要素】

B: *It's all right, Mr. Black. Really, I don't mind at all. Besides, I can use a little extra money. My husband's birthday is next month. I want to buy him a new watch.*

A: *What kind are you going to get him, a Bulova?*

B: *No, I thought I'd get a Rolex. Or an Elgin. I don't really know much about watches.*

A: *I've got one of those Seiko digitals*『数字型手表』*. I really like it.*

B: *Do you think my husband would like one like that?*

A: *I'm sure he would. The only problem is that they're a little bit heavy.*

B: *If they're that good, I think I'll go ahead and get him one.*

A: *Well at least he won't get a tie. That's what I usually get.*

B: *Remember, it's the thought*『关心；挂念』*that counts* 『重要；起作用；有价值』*.*

【李阳·克立兹三最口腔肌肉训练记录为：45秒】

【李阳·克立兹一口气底气训练记录为:不到4口气】

40. Q: What is Jean doing now?

    A: Typing letters for Mrs. Grant.

41. Q: Where is Mr. Black going?

    A: Chicago.

42. Q: When will Jean finish the report?

    A: By 8:00.

43. What kind of watch is Jean going to buy?

    A: A Seiko.

第 二 套

Part A

1. She used to live in the dormitory, but now she has her own apartment.

   = She has moved out of the dormitory.

2. We'll probably be late for the concert, won't we?

   = I think we'll miss the beginning of the concert.

3. I'd better not go to bed because I haven't finished my chemistry assignment.

   = I have to stay up『不睡;熬夜』to finish my chemistry.

4. I always forget people's names at parties.

   = It's hard for me to remember a person's name at a party.

5. You gave me the right address for Bill's apartment, didn't you?

   = I hope you gave me Bill's correct address.

6. *Just down the street is a nice little gift shop.*

   = There is a gift shop『1 礼品店』nearby.

7. *The snack bar has fresh fruit, right?*

   = Doesn't the snack『快餐；小吃』bar sell fresh fruit?

8. *There are big sales going on in the department stores downtown this week according to Charlie.*

   = Charlie told us about the sales『大减价』in the stores downtown.

9. *There's not a single cloud in the sky this afternoon!*

   = It's a sunny day today.

10. *Not one student in my class has studied painting before.*

    = Nobody in the class has ever had any painting lessons.

    （没有人学习过绘画。）

11. *Behind the lecture hall is a small parking lot.*

    = The lecture hall is in front of a parking lot『停车场』.

12. *Lucy was offered a scholarship by the university that was her first choice.*

    = Lucy got a scholarship to the university of her choice.

13. *Barbara discovered she was ineligible『不合格的；没有资格的』for the song contest.*

    = She found out she couldn't enter the contest.

14. *Ted once worked there, but no longer does.*

    = He doesn't work there anymore.

15. She replaced 『替换』 **the broken pane** 『窗格玻璃』 **of glass.**

= She fixed the window.

16. I guessed the right answer.

= I got the correct answer by chance.

17. I've promised to take Stone some of this delicious tea.

= I said I'd take some of this tea to Stone.

18. Mary Anne! That's who makes the best soup.

= Mary Ann makes outstanding 『著名的；优秀的；杰出的』soup.

19. The last person I want to see is Jeff! 【高级精品句】

= I don't want to see Jeff at all.

20. Sarah used to teach psychology 『心理学』, **but now she's a corporate** 『市政府的；公司的』 **statistician** 『统计工作者』.

= Sarah has a different job now.

Part B

21. A: Could you tell me something about the apartment you're renting?

B: Well. It's 285 dollars a month including heat.

Q: What does the woman want to do?

A: Get some information.

[ˌplænəˈtɛriəm]

22. A: The planetarium's 『天文馆』 **new show on space stations is pretty interesting.**

B: Pretty interesting! I could spend hours there.

Q: What does the man say about the show?

A: He found it fascinating『迷人的；吸引人的』.

23. *A: Did you hear that Greg got a job in his uncle's law office?*

    B: Like they say-It's who you know that counts『重要；有价值』.

    Q: What does the man mean?

    A: Greg only got the job because of his uncle.

24. *A: I think I've got this experiment set up right now.*

    B: You only think it's right? In Chemistry you've got to be sure.

    Q: What is the woman suggesting to the man?

    A: He must be extremely careful.

25. *A: Is your roommate looking forward to going home for the Summer?*

    B: She's counting the days.

    Q: What can be inferred about the woman's roommate?

    A: She's excited about going home.
       (她为回家而激动。)

26. *A: I thought I'd take the half-day tour*『半日游』of the city.

    B: Why not the whole day?

    Q: What does the man suggest the woman do?

    A: Take a longer tour.

27. *A: You look tired. Can I help you with those boxes?*

    B: Thanks——but they weigh a ton each!

    Q: What is the man implying?

    A: The boxes might be too heavy for her to lift.

28. A: *How did you like the president's speech tonight?*

(你觉得总统的演说怎么样？)

B: *Unfortunately I got home too late to watch it.*

Q: *What are these people talking about?*

A: *A speech on television.*

29. A: *Do you want me to take the book back for you?*

B: *When you have a chance.*

Q: *What will the man probably do?*

A: *Return the book.*

30. A: *I've been taking four courses── but I think I'll drop one of them at the end of this term.*

B: *That may be for the best『结果是最好的』.*

Q: *What does the woman mean?*

A: *The man's idea is probably a good one.*

31. A: *Miss, can you give me change『零钱』 for a dollar?*

B: *I'm sorry, sir. I'm not allowed to give change without a purchase. If you go across the hall, you'll find a change machine in front of the jewelry store.*

Q: *Where does the woman suggest that the man get change?*

A: *From a machine.*

【李阳·克立兹三最口腔肌肉训练记录为：**9**秒】

32. A: *Judy earned a lot of money over the summer as a consultant for that agency.*

B: *I don't doubt it. What surprises me is that she's still working there now that classes have started again.*

Q: *What does the man say about Judy?*

A: *He wonders why she's kept her job.*

【李阳·克立兹三最口腔肌肉训练记录为：9秒】

33. A: *Rita can certainly play the piano well!*

    B: *Oh! You have heard her play.*

    （你原来是听过她弹钢琴啊！）

    Q: *What had the woman assumed about the man?*

    A: *He hadn't heard Rita play the piano.*

34. A: <u>*You're not much of*</u>『算不上；称不上；不是什么了不起的』 <u>*a Rock and Roll*</u> *fan, are you?*

    B: *It's far from*『远非；绝非』*being my favorite kind of music, that's for sure.*

    （它远远不是我喜欢的音乐，这是毫无疑问的。）

    Q: *What does the man imply?*

    A: *He doesn't like rock'n roll.*

35. A: *Would you mind if we discussed tomorrow's a-genda*『议程；讨论事项』*before dinner this evening?*

    B: *Not at all. I certainly don't want to talk about it during our meal!*

    Q: *When will they probably discuss the agenda?*

    A: *Before dinner.*【接待外国朋友时常用】

    【李阳·克立兹三最口腔肌肉训练记录为：8秒】

Part C

Questions 36-41 are based on the following conversation.

A: *Lucille, I've been admiring*『喜欢；欣赏；羡慕』*that* <u>*sculpture*</u>『雕刻；雕塑』*you have on your desk. It looks like a Polar bear*『北极熊』*.*

B: *That's right. It is a Polar bear. It was made out of soapstone*『皂石』 *by an Inuit artist from Northern Canada. The dark grey stone is easy to carve*『雕刻』 *and lines which look almost white in contrast can be made with hand tools.*

A: *I've seen other Inuit sculptures made from whalebone*『鲸骨』 *and wood. You can see by looking at this bear that the style seems quite abstract*『抽象的』*, and yet there's a realistic impression of the bear's shape and stance*『姿态』.

B: *Inuit sculptors usually do depict*『刻画；描绘』*animals in just such a style. Their favorite subjects are the animals of Northern Canada and Alaska like Polar bears, seals*『海豹』*, Caribou*『北美的驯鹿』*, and whales. The Inuit hunt some of these animals for food.*

A: *Yes, I know. But the polar bear is their favorite because of its size, strength, and agility*『动作敏捷；机敏』*.*

B: *That's true. They recognize*『公认；承认』*it as one of the most graceful* 『优美的；雅致的』*swimmers and fishers of all animals. And most important, the polar bear symbolizes*『象征；代表』*all the skills the Inuit hunters expect of themselves for survival.*

【李阳·克立兹三最口腔肌肉训练记录为：50 秒】
【李阳·克立兹一口气底气训练记录为：4 口气】

36. Q: Where does this conversation probably take place?
    A: In an office.

37. Q: According to the conversation, in what part of Canada does the artist live?
    A: Northern.

38. Q: What kind of art object are the people looking at?
    A: A stone sculpture.

39. Q: How does the man describe the appearance of the object being discussed?

A: Both abstract and realistic.

40. Q: Which animal do the Inuit people admire most?

A: The polar bear.

41. Q: What does the Inuit's favourite animal symbolize to them?

A: Survival skills.

第 三 套

Part A

1. How about going for a walk with us?

= Let's all go out for a walk.

2. If I'd been more careful, I wouldn't have lost it.
【王牌精品句】

= I lost it because I wasn't careful.

3. Look where you are going!

= I wish you'd look where you are walking.

4. Mary had the waitress check the bill.

= Mary told the waitress to go over『仔细检查』the bill.

5. Never have I been so embarrassed『窘迫;困惑;为难;局促不安』.

（我从来没有这么尴尬过。）【高级精品句】

= I was more embarrassed than ever before.

126

6. Bob ran into『偶然碰见』an old friend at school.

= Bob unexpectedly『料想不到地;意外地』met an old friend at school.

7. **You are expected to select a major by your junior year.**

   = You should have chosen your major by your junior year.

8. **Our chemistry class is far more interesting than it used to be.**

   = Our chemistry class is more interesting than it once was.

   （我们现在的化学课比以前有趣得多。）

   【李阳·克立兹三最口腔肌肉训练记录为:4秒】

9. **I got lost as I had misread『读错』the directions.**

   = I couldn't find the way because I misread the directions.

10. **Barbara isn't used to working so early in the morning.** = It's an unaccustomedly『不平常地』early hour for Barbara to be working.

11. **The deadline『限期；截止日期』 for applications is June 1st.**

    = The last day to apply is June 1st.

12. **John told me that you should study harder.**

    = John said you ought to study harder.

13. **I'll be ready to leave as soon as I pack『打点行李；装箱』.** = I can go when I've finished packing.

14. **There were quite a few『相当多的』people in the line.**

    = A lot of people were in the line.

15. **Betty was impatient『不耐烦的；急躁的』and insisted**

127

they leave immediately.

= Betty was restless『烦乱的；坐立不安的』and wanted to leave.

16. ***He gave a very original***『新颖的；有独创性的』 ***presentation, don't you think?***

= I think his presentation『演讲；发表；展示；上演；提出』was quite different, don't you?

17. ***Dale couldn't find a blue tie, so he bought a black one instead.***

= There were no blue ties so he bought a black one.

18. ***They had to leave before the end of the game.***

= They left before the game finished.

19. ***Whoever wrote that must have lived in New York.***
(写那个的人一定在纽约生活过。)【高级精品句】

= Only someone who has lived in New York could have written that.
(只有在纽约生活过的人才可能写出那样的东西。)

20. ***The university administers***『管理；执行』 ***several awards on the basis of achievement.***

= Based on achievement several awards are given by the university.

上册完
请继续攻击下册！
祝您成功！